WIMBLEDON
Gentlemen's Singles Champions
1877–2005

WIMBLEDON
Gentlemen's Singles Champions
1877–2005

John Barrett and Alan Little

**WIMBLEDON
LAWNTENNIS
MUSEUM**

Published in 2006 by
Wimbledon Lawn Tennis Museum
All England Lawn Tennis Club
Church Road, Wimbledon
London, SW19 5AE

A CIP catalogue record for this book
is available from the British Library

ISBN 0 906741 42 4

Designed by Roger Walker
Typeset in Bembo and Optima

Printed and bound in Great Britain by
L&S Printing Company Limited,
Worthing, West Sussex

FRONTISPIECE
Trendsetter William Renshaw, seven times champion; Australia's Norman Brookes,
the first overseas male champion; Fred Perry, Britain's triple-winner and the first to win
all four Grand Slam titles; Sweden's superstar Bjorn Borg, whose five successive titles
are still a modern record.

Contents

Preface

The first edition of this publication appeared in 1986, two years after the booklet which had recorded the achievements of the Lady Champions.

Following the updating and republication of the latter volume in 2005 by the Wimbledon Lawn Tennis Museum, this new edition covering the Gentlemen's Champions follows in 2006.

As with the ladies, the original text for the biographical sketches provided by that doyen of tennis writers, the late Lance Tingay of the *Daily Telegraph*, has been revised and updated. The later biographies, from Boris Becker onwards, have been provided by John Barrett, BBC TV's senior tennis commentator and tennis correspondent of the *Financial Times* since 1963.

Once again Alan Little, Honorary Librarian of the Wimbledon Lawn Tennis Museum, has cheerfully shouldered the burden of providing the detailed statistics of each player's career which follow the biographical sketches. It should be noted that the facts and figures refer to performances up to the end of 2005.

The publishers would like to thank the award-winning photographer Mr Michael Cole whose historic pictures, together with those of his late father Arthur, have been widely used in both the Gentlemen's and Ladies' publications.

June 2006

PASSING THE BATON

Three time former champion Boris Becker (right) hands the trophy to Pete Sampras after the American had beaten him in the 1995 final to win the third of his seven titles.

The Gentlemen's Singles Champions

To keen followers of lawn tennis the names are household words, respected and revered for their supreme achievements. They are the Wimbledon champions.

But how did it all begin? It was on a damp Thursday in 1877, July 19th to be precise, that Spencer Gore, a good games player at Harrow and a keen cricketer all his life, became winner of The Lawn Tennis Championship at the newly renamed *All England Croquet and Lawn Tennis Club*, Wimbledon, where tennis had been adopted only two years earlier. Gore was a surveyor aged 27 years 131 days and a local resident. He was the best of 22 challengers and assured of lawn tennis immortality as the first in a very distinguished line.

Since his pioneer triumph 61 other men have emulated him. They range in age from the precocious Boris Becker, a mere 17 years 227 days on the day of his first success in 1985, to the stalwart Arthur Gore (no relation to Spencer) who was 41 years 182 days old when he won for the third time in 1909. Of these 62 worthies 35 have won just once. America's Pete Sampras won seven times in eight years during the 1990s, a total first achieved by William Renshaw one hundred years earlier. However, in Renshaw's day the champion each year stood out until the Challenge Round where he played the winner of the All Comers Singles for the title. Accordingly, in compiling his seven wins Renshaw played just 18 matches. Sampras played 49.

The United States has provided most champions. There have been 21 in all, the first – 'Big Bill' Tilden in 1920. There have been 12 Australians, with Norman Brookes the first antipodean and the first overseas winner in 1907. Fourteen have been British (of whom three were Irish) but the only champion since 1909 was Fred Perry, a triple winner in 1934, '35 and '66.

Nearly all were great players, some very great indeed. To be the Wimbledon singles champion is perhaps the ultimate test of greatness. One or two needed a measure of luck to acquire their status; even the greatest had to avoid bad luck, for that is the way of the game.

Spencer Gore (whose brother was a notable Bishop of Birmingham) became champion just 47 days after the All England Club committee had authorised the novelty. Dr Henry Jones, Julian Marshall and C.G. Heathcote speedily organised the tournament out of nothing. There were no standard rules and they had to decide on the shape of the court and its size, the height of the net, and which scoring system to adopt. To their eternal credit they chose the *real tennis* system of scoring, which has survived to this day, rather than the *rackets* system with games of fifteen points. What they decreed basically became the rules of lawn tennis that are still in use today, with but minor changes.

Wimbledon's record as the premier event has shone undimmed over the years to the 2005 meeting when The Championships were staged for the 119th time. Wimbledon has long been a British institution. Among the world's most famous sporting events one would hesitate to claim that its happenings reverberated more loudly round the world than the World Cup of soccer or the Olympic Games; but Wimbledon may stand alongside with equal dignity.

The gentlemen who have contributed vitally to the prestige of The Lawn Tennis Championships are honoured and remembered in this volume. Their achievements are collated, the figures totalled. As to the best, that is a matter of opinion. The statistics can be used to bolster, or confound, an argument on such a theme. As long as lawn tennis is played the Wimbledon Gentlemen's singles champions will live in the hall of fame.

Nine of the immortals won at their first attempt – Spencer Gore in 1877, Frank Hadow in 1878, John Hartley in 1879, Gerald Patterson in 1919, Bill Tilden in 1920, Ellsworth Vines in 1932, Bobby Riggs in 1939, Ted Schroeder in 1949 and Richard Savitt in 1951. Hadow, Riggs and Schroeder never played at Wimbledon again.

Calculating from 1922, when all had to play through, Jack Kramer was the easiest winner in 1947 in that he lost only 22.15 per cent of his games. But he lost one set. Don Budge in 1938 did not lose a set and nor did Tony Trabert in 1955, Charles McKinley in 1963, and Bjorn Borg in 1976. Champions who won after being within one shot, or more, of losing at some stage were William Renshaw in 1889, Wilfred Baddeley in 1895, Arthur Gore in 1901, Bill Tilden in 1921, Henri Cochet in 1927, Bob Falkenburg in 1948, Ted Schroeder in 1949 and Neale Fraser in 1960.

The pages that follow are dedicated to the memory of some truly remarkable athletes whose exploits on Wimbledon's historic Centre Court have become part of the folklore of our sport.

Spencer Gore

1877

The Pioneer

Spencer Gore became the first Wimbledon Champion when, on Thursday 19th July 1877 at some time after half past four he beat William Marshall by 6–1 6–2 6–4. It was his fifth match since the start of the tournament ten days earlier and had been postponed from the Monday because of rain. Gore beat all his rivals fairly comfortably, losing a set in only two rounds.

His style of play provoked some comment. Was it not unfair that he should strike the ball before it bounced – and sometimes before it had actually crossed the net, then five feet high at the posts and three feet three inches high in the middle? In that first Championship there were no rules to cover such matters.

Gore, an old Harrovian who was born and lived in Wimbledon, was a zealous games player. He had played rackets at school. He was also a cricketer. Indeed cricket was his main enthusiasm and he went on playing it all his life. As for the new game of lawn tennis, at which he was the inaugural champion, he did not think much of it. He later wrote:

> 'That anyone who has really played well at cricket, tennis, or even rackets, will ever seriously give his attention to lawn tennis, beyond showing himself to be a promising player, is extremely doubtful; for in all probability the monotony of the game as compared with others would choke him off before he had time to excel in it'.

Even if feeling no warmth for the game Gore was sportsman enough to defend his title one year later. As was the custom in those days he stood out as champion until the challenge round. There he met Frank Hadow who had the wit to hoist the ball over the oncoming volleyer. Since Gore had not learnt to smash the ploy was effective and Hadow displaced him as champion. And that, so far as the records go, was the last seen of Spencer Gore in the game. He died, only 56 years old, in 1906. But as champion he stands above all others. He was the first.

Wimbledon Singles Record:
1877, won 5 matches, *champion* (sets 15–2; games 99–46).
1878, won 0 matches, lost Frank Hadow, Challenge Round.

Matches: 5–1; sets 15–5; games 112–68

Longest Match: 3 matches of 35 games.

Age on winning singles: 27 years 131 days.

Career Achievements:
The Championships, Wimbledon: singles 1877.

Full name: Spencer William Gore
Born: 10th March, 1850, Wimbledon, Surrey, England.
Died: 19th April, 1906, Ramsgate, Kent, England.

Frank Hadow

1878

A Fleeting Success

If Spencer Gore was a champion who did not think much of the game his successor in the role of champion, Frank Hadow, was a sportsman who happened to be passing by.

An old Harrovian, he had become a tea planter in Ceylon, as Sri Lanka was then called. He came back on leave for the summer of 1878 and was induced to play the novel game of lawn tennis. He grew keen enough to enter, together with his brother, the Wimbledon Championships.

He had more tactical acumen than most. Although feeling far from well for most of the time – probably the effects of some eastern 'bug' he had acquired – he saw no future, when it came to the Challenge Round, of trying to pass the volleying Gore down the line over the high part of the net which, though lowered from the year before, was four feet nine inches high. So he lobbed. Two of the three sets were close and, since the title was at stake, advantage sets were played.

Hadow's defence triumphed by 7–5 6–1 9–7. Hadow won his championship without losing a set in any round. He stands now as the only man never to have lost a set in the Wimbledon Championships. He went back to Ceylon and never returned. Not, that is, until the Jubilee Celebrations of 1926 when he was prevailed upon to come along and receive his champion's medal. He had not been back to Wimbledon since his triumph in 1878. Nor, in the interval, had he ever seen a first class lawn tennis match.

Wimbledon Singles Record:
1878, won 6 matches *champion* (sets 18–0; games 112–47).

Matches: As above.

Longest Match: Challenge Round 1878, beat Spencer Gore 7–5 6–1 9–7 – a total of 35 games.

Age on winning singles: 23 years 175 days.

Career Achievements:
The Championships, Wimbledon: singles 1878.

Full name: Patrick Francis Hadow
Born: 24th January, 1855, Regent's Park, Middlesex, England.
Died: 29th June, 1946, Bridgewater, Somerset, England.

Rev. John Hartley

1879, 1880

The Vicar of Play

The third winner of the singles at Wimbledon was rather more than the third old Harrovian to take the crown. He might be described as the last of the vicarage lawn type of player to win; it was his successor as champion who propelled lawn tennis into the aggressive style of play it has had ever since.

Appropriately he was a vicar, the Reverend John Hartley, an Oxford graduate whose living was at Dumeston in the North Riding of Yorkshire. He was 33 when he first won and, unlike his predecessors, he had been a real tennis rather than a rackets player. His style was essentially defensive. He took the ball late and he stayed at the back of the court, relying on his persistence of return.

The crowning irony of his initial victory in 1879 was in the man he beat in the title match. Since Hadow was not there to defend in a Challenge Round, this was the final of the All Comers' Singles. He was Vere St. Leger Goold whose identity was for years hidden under the pseudonym of 'St. Leger'.

Goold was an Irishman. He had, in fact, won the inaugural Irish Championship a few weeks earlier. He was reputedly rather a wild sort of player. Certainly Hartley was too steady for him and had no problems in winning in three sets. The fact that the match was played at all was the upshot of some hectic travelling by the worthy Hartley. When he entered the Championships he did not visualise reaching the last stages. Consequently he found himself due to play the last match on the Monday when he had made no provision for the Sunday duties at his church. He had to travel about 250 miles to north Yorkshire and then, rising at the crack of dawn on the Monday, hurry down by train to Kings Cross, then from Waterloo on the London and South Western Railway to Wimbledon.

The irony of it? John Hartley was the only beneficed clergyman to be Wimbledon Champion. The man he beat for the title was later charged with murder. That was in 1907 when, following a trial, both Goold and his wife were convicted of the murder of a Danish widow in Monte Carlo. The saint and the sinner?

Wimbledon Singles Record:
1879, won 6 matches, *champion* (sets 18–4; games 119–66).
1880, won 1 match, *champion* (sets 3–1; games 20–14).
1881, won 0 matches, lost William Renshaw, Challenge Round.
1882, did not play.
1883, won 1 match, lost Herbert Wilberforce, 2nd round.

Matches: 8–2; sets 25–11; games 176–125.

Longest Match: 2nd round 1879, beat Lestocq Erskine 6–4 6–5 5–6 0–6 6–5 – a total of 49 games.

Age on first winning singles: 30 years 187 days.

Age on last winning singles: 31 years 188 days.

Career Achievements:
The Championships, Wimbledon: singles 1879, 1880.

Full name: Reverend John Thorneycroft Hartley
Born: 9th January, 1849, Tong, Shifnal, Shropshire, England.
Died: 21st August, 1935, Knaresborough, Yorkshire, England.

William Renshaw

1881–1886, 1889

Champion of Champions

If any player merits description as the founding father of the game as played today it is the fourth of the Wimbledon Champions, William Renshaw. He developed a strong overhead service – though he was not the first to serve that way – a punishing smash (for years the term 'Renshaw smash' was part of the game's vocabulary) and he took the ball early and hit it hard. He transformed the defensive slice and cut of the vicarage lawn into the modern style.

Renshaw was a wealthy young man. He had what today would be called charisma. Both his high skill and warmth of personality took the game to new dimensions. During his reign the Wimbledon crowds increased apace. The London and South Western Railway built a special halt by the side of the All England Lawn Tennis Club and ran special excursions. He was twin with Ernest, who was the younger, and had equal appeal. The record shows that William was the better, though each was well in front of all rivals.

William was 20 when he won at his second attempt. The soft balling of Hartley presented no problems in the one-sided Challenge Round of 1881. In the next two years he was unsuccessfully challenged by his brother and while they had long matches neither was inspired to play his best against the other. Then he thrice thrust back Herbert Lawford, who assiduously wielded a famous forehand in vain. With six wins behind him William did not defend in 1887. The next year he lost to Willoby Hamilton, a steady and intelligent performer, who alone was able to weaken the champion's confidence.

William's last triumph was in 1889 and it was after one of the most notable matches of all time. In the All Comers' final William played Harry Barlow, a man always to the forefront. William lost the first two sets, but salvaged the third in the 14th game. In the fourth Barlow was six times at match point. At 6–7 30–40, William faced the certainty of defeat, for he dropped his racket. With an open court

Barlow made the grand gesture. He merely dollied the ball to give his opponent time to recover. Was there ever a greater act of sportsmanship?

William's adventures were not over even after taking that set 10–8. He fell behind to love–5 in the fifth set, then he hauled up to 6–5 and finally won the match 3–6 5–7 8–6 10–8 8–6. It was the longest match had by William at Wimbledon. His defeat of brother Ernest in the Challenge Round was the most one sided of their title clashes, albeit over four sets.

Thus William won the singles for the seventh time. Six times in a row, then number seven, a feat unequalled until the American, Pete Sampras, won seven in the 1990s. A year later his old *bête noire*, Hamilton, deposed him. A decade of greatness had finished.

The period of the Renshaws coincided with the growth of the game in the United States and its rivalry with the British. In 1883 the Clark brothers, Clarence and Joseph, came to England as a representative American pair. Their challenge was taken up by the Renshaws and the first Anglo-American contest was staged at the All England Club in Worple Road on July 18th. The Renshaws won 6–4

8–6 3–6 6–1. Five days later they won again, this time by 6–3 6–2 6–3.

The Renshaws were the 'modern' pair. They advanced to the net in unison. The Clarks played one up, one back. This was perhaps the only time when US doubles tactics were found wanting against the British.

The twins came from Leamington and went to school at Cheltenham. As infants they were involved in a friendly law suit against one another to settle the problem occasioned by their twinship in their father's will.

Neither was long lived but William died five years after his brother when he was 43. When William began playing lawn tennis it was a pastime. He turned it into a sport.

Wimbledon Singles Record:
1880, won 2 matches, lost Otway Woodhouse, 3rd round.
1881, won 7 matches, *champion* (sets 21–3; games 136–58).
1882, won 1 match, *champion* (sets 3–2; games 24–17).
1883, won 1 match, *champion* (sets 3–2; games 24–21).
1884, won 1 match, *champion* (sets 3–0; games 21–11).
1885, won 1 match, *champion* (sets 3–1; games 24–18).
1886, won 1 match, *champion* (sets 3–1; games 23–14).
1887, did not play.
1888, won 2 matches, lost Willoughby Hamilton, quarter-final.
1889, won 6 matches, *champion* (sets 18–4; games 135–90).
1890, won 0 matches, lost Willoughby Hamilton, Challenge Round.

Matches: 22–3; sets 70–23; games 524–350.

Longest Match: All Comers' Final 1889, beat Harry Barlow 3–6 5–7 8–6 10–8 8–6 – a total of 67 games.

Age on first winning singles: 20 years 191 days.

Age on last winning singles: 28 years 186 days.

Overall Record:

	Titles	*Matches*		
	Titles	*Played*	*Won*	*Lost*
Singles	7	25	22	3
Doubles	5	15	14	1
Mixed	0	0	0	0
	12	40	36	4

Career Achievements:
The Championships, Wimbledon: singles 1881–1886, 1889; doubles 1884–1886, 1888, 1889.
Oxford Doubles Championship: 1880, 1881.
Irish Championships: singles 1880–1882; doubles 1881, 1883–1885.

Full name: William Charles Renshaw
Born: 3rd January, 1861, Leamington, Warwickshire, England.
Died: 12th August, 1904, Swanage, Dorset, England.

Herbert Lawford

1887

Forehand Fantastic

If lawn tennis had not been taken so far forward by the Renshaw twins the champion to have bridged the gap between the vicarage lawn and the modern game would have been Herbert Fortescue Lawford, a product of Repton and Edinburgh.

He was 27 years old when he competed for the first time. That was as early as 1878. It took him nine years to get his eventual success. Originally the soft balling of Canon Hartley confounded him. Later either William Renshaw or his twin Ernest was too skillful. From 1884 to 1886 Lawford was unbeaten in the All Comers' singles, only to have to yield in the Challenge Round to William. The next year, 1887, William did not defend and Lawford broke through at last. In the title match, the All Comers' final, he beat Ernest in five sets. The same player got his revenge in the Challenge Round twelve months later.

Lawford was 36 years old when champion and as well known on the courts as the Renshaws. He was distinctive in his hooped jersey and cap, white knickerbockers and long black socks. His forehand was even more distinctive. He hit it faster than most using a western grip and top spin. 'The Lawford Stroke' was known and feared by all opponents. He took the ball at the top of the bound.

Had the Renshaws not existed it is overwhelmingly probable that Lawford would have won The Championship not just once but eight times. He was competing for the tenth time when he did win.

In 1885 he had the distinction of being the first British Covered Court Champion. Prior to that he twice won, in 1880 and 1883, the Princes' Club

Championship, a tournament which for four brief years threatened to rival Wimbledon in prestige.

Lawford was one of the pioneers who took the game forward.

Wimbledon Singles Record:
1878, won 2 matches, lost Lestocq Erskine, semi-final.
1879, won 0 matches, lost Eric Lubbock, 1st round.
1880, won 6 matches, lost John Hartley, Challenge Round.
1881, won 3 matches, lost William Renshaw, semi-final, (lost Richard Richardson 3rd place).
1882, won 3 matches, lost Ernest Renshaw, semi-final.
1883, won 0 matches, lost Ernest Renshaw, 1st round.
1884, won 4 matches, lost William Renshaw, Challenge Round.
1885, won 4 matches, lost William Renshaw, Challenge Round.
1886, won 4 matches, lost William Renshaw, Challenge Round.
1887, won 4 matches, *champion* (sets 12–3; games 86–60).
1888, won 0 matches, lost Ernest Renshaw, Challenge Round.
1889, won 2 matches, lost William Renshaw, semi-final.

Matches: 33–12; sets 112–50; games 827–631 (including 3rd place match 1881).

Longest Match: 3rd place 1881, lost to Richard Richardson 3–6 6–4 1–6 6–3 5–7 and 1st round 1883, lost to Ernest Renshaw 6–5 1–6 6–3 2–6 5–7 – a total of 47 games.

Age on winning singles: 36 years 53 days.

Overall Record:

	Titles	Matches		
		Played	Won	Lost
Singles	1	44	33	11
Doubles	0	1	0	1
Mixed	0	0	0	0
Total	1	45	33	12

Career Achievements:
The Championships, Wimbledon: singles 1887.
Oxford Doubles Championship: 1879.
Irish Championships: singles 1884–1886.

Full name: Herbert Fortescue Lawford
Born: 15th May, 1851, Bayswater, Middlesex, England.
Died: 20th April, Dess, Aberdeenshire, Scotland.

Ernest Renshaw

1888

The Younger Genius

Of the two Renshaws Ernest was said to have been the more graceful but the less penetrating. William had the dash. Ernest had the fluency. William was the terrier, never still. Ernest was the panther. But it seems certain that Ernest took second place to no player save his elder twin and if William had not been there to win the title then Ernest would have carried it off.

They disliked playing each other and never produced much of a match when they did. Ernest, it was said, did not give his best on such occasions. Even so in their three meetings in the Challenge Round at Wimbledon William needed five sets to gain the victory on two occasions and four sets in the other.

When Ernest got his sole singles victory, in 1888, it was after William had been eliminated by his *bête noire* as an opponent, the Irishman, Willoby Hamilton. Ernest avenged that loss in the semi-final, the stage at which he would have expected to meet William.

The Wimbledon crowds of the 1880s saw more of Ernest since he was playing through the field while the more successful William was standing out until the Challenge Round. In doubles they shared the glory and were, at Wimbledon, invincible.

Ernest did not live to see the new century; lawn tennis in the twentieth century would not have been the same had it not been for his example and that of his more dominant twin.

Wimbledon Singles Record:
1880, won 3 matches, lost Otway Woodhouse, quarter-final.
1881, won 2 matches, lost Richard Richardson, 3rd round.
1882, won 5 matches, lost William Renshaw, Challenge Round.

1883, won 4 matches, lost William Renshaw, Challenge Round.
1884, won 3 matches, Charles Grinstead, semi-final.
1885, won 4 matches, lost Herbert Lawford, All Comer's Final.
1886, won 2 matches, lost Ernest Lewis, quarter-final.
1887, won 2 matches, lost Herbert Lawford, All Comers' Final.
1888, won 5 matches, *champion* (sets 15–4; games 117–78).
1889, won 0 matches, lost William Renshaw, Challenge Round.
1890, did not play.
1891, won 2 matches, lost Wilfred Baddeley, semi-final.
1892, did not play.
1893, won 0 matches, lost Harold Mahony, 2nd round.

Matches: 32–11; sets 112–52; games 848–636.

Longest Match: Semi-final 1885, beat Ernest Browne 6–4 8–6 2–6 5–7 6–4 – a total of 54 games.

Age on winning singles: 27 years 195 days.

Overall Record:

	Titles	Matches		
		Played	Won	Lost
Singles	1	43	32	11
Doubles	5	16	15	1
Mixed	0	0	0	0
Total	6	59	47	12

Career Achievements:
The Championships, Wimbledon: singles 1888; doubles 1884–1886, 1888, 1889.
Oxford Doubles Championships: 1880, 1881.
Irish Championships: singles 1883, 1887, 1888; 1892; doubles 1881, 1883–1885.

Full name: James Ernest Renshaw
Born: 3rd January, 1861, Leamington, Warwickshire, England.
Died: 2nd September, 1899, Twyford, Berkshire, England.

Willoby Hamilton

1890

Ireland's First

If William Renshaw was indis-
putably the best of his time it is
equally certain that the one man
against whom he was never confident was Willoby Hamilton. He
always had the soft answer which
turned away Renshaw's majestic
wrath.

He beat William when the then
six times champion came back from
a year's absence in 1888. Twin
Ernest got his revenge and beat
Hamilton in the next round.

Hamilton's triumph came two
years later. William, having taken
the title for the seventh time by
beating his twin in the Challenge
Round, was in defence of a title
once more. Hamilton had a hard
time in taking himself to the title

match. Wilfred Baddeley, who was to be champion in the future, he coped with
easily enough. Joshua Pim, another future champion and another Irishman, took an
opening love set against him in the semi-finals of the All Comers'. The redoubtable
Harry Barlow took him to all of five hard sets, with the fifth going to 7–5, before
Hamilton hoisted himself into the Challenge Round.

There the famous William, now 29 and giving away four years, was enmeshed
yet again in the careful web of patient accuracy spun by Hamilton. Despite a lead
of two sets to one, Renshaw failed to win for the eighth time. Hamilton won his
title by taking the last two sets 6–1 6–1. Hamilton had crowned a career of patience
and craft and his ambitions were satisfied. He did not defend a year later.

Such was the first of the Irish victories. It was, of course, all one in those days;
English or Irish or Scottish or Welsh, the national identity was of the British Isles.
Even so they took note of the Wimbledon happenings that year in Dublin for Pim

and Stoker, Irishmen both, took the doubles. And the women's singles, albeit not the best over the years with an entry of but four, had Lena Rice from Tipperary as the victor.

So, led by Hamilton, Ireland had a clean sweep of all the titles. One hardly doubt but they sank a jar or two at the Fitzwilliam Club on that occasion.

Hamilton was far from robust. His sobriquet was 'The Ghost'. Ill health forced him to give up lawn tennis after winning the Wimbledon singles. Nonetheless he did not die until he was nearly 79. In his young days he played soccer for Ireland.

Wimbledon Singles Record:
1886, won 1 match, lost Herbert Lawford, quarter-final.
1887, did not play.
1888, won 3 matches, lost Ernest Renshaw, semi-final.
1889, won 1 match, lost Harry Barlow, semi-final.
1890, won 6 matches, *champion* (sets 18–5; games 125–72).

Matches: 11–3; sets 36–18; games 293–223.

Longest Match: Quarter-final 1889, beat Ernest Lewis 4–6 7–5 6–3 5–7 6–4 – a total of 53 games.

Age on winning singles: 25 years 210 days.

Overall Record:

	Titles	Matches		
		Played	Won	Lost
Singles	1	14	11	3
Doubles	0	0	0	0
Mixed	0	0	0	0
Total	1	14	11	3

Career Achievements:
The Championships, Wimbledon: singles 1890.
Irish Championships: singles 1889; doubles 1886–1888.

Full name: Willoby James Hamilton
Born: 9th December, 1864, Monasterevin, Co. Kildare, Ireland.
Died: 27th September, 1943, Dundrum, Dublin, Ireland.

Wilfred Baddeley

1891, 1892, 1895

The Young Champion

The eighth man to inscribe his name on the roll of Wimbledon singles champions, Wilfred Baddeley, was 19 years 174 days old when he did so for the first time on Saturday 4th July 1891 and until 1985 no younger man had done so. Nor was there a younger holder of the US singles title.

The precocious champion was a twin and he and brother Herbert threatened to dominate the 1890s as the Renshaw twins had dominated the 1880s. Just as William, the elder twin, was the stronger player so was Wilfred, the elder among the Baddeleys. Wilfred won the singles three times in all, Herbert never looked like doing as well, though he was three times a semi-finalist in the All Comers' event. As a partnership they took the doubles four times.

Wilfred Baddeley had his triumphs after the Renshaws and before the Doherty brothers, Reggie and Laurie, took command. Wimbledon's standard at that time fell to what were rather low levels. Indeed the decline, once the Renshaws had ceased to cast their magic spell, was such that in 1895, when Wilfred won his third and last singles, the Lawn Tennis Championships produced a loss of £33 to the All England Club. There was even talk at that time of the All England Club being taken over by Queen's Club!

Wilfred was small of stature and famous for his consistency. It was said that he had never missed a sitter in his life; but he lacked power and severity. The key to his initial Wimbledon victory in 1891 was his semi-final win against an appallingly off-form Ernest Renshaw. Baddeley beat him 6–0 6–1 6–1 in an alleged half hour. If indeed the match did take but 30 minutes it must rank as about the fastest best of five sets match of all time. But timing records have often been vague.

The All Comers' Final against Joshua Pim was enough to give Wilfred the title, for Hamilton was not defending. A year later Wilfred beat Pim again, this time in the Challenge Round. In 1893 they played their third title match in as many years when Pim was a winner in four sets. Then Wilfred played through in 1894 to lose again to Pim in their fourth clash in four years.

The Baddeley twins, Wilfred (right) and Herbert (left). Wilfred won the title three times, but Herbert was never as good a singles player.

By this time Pim had mastered Wilfred Baddeley but his fellow Irishman did not play in 1895 and the two times champion made it three. Wilfred's 1895 success was notable for his walk-over in the semi-final. It was against his twin – from whom he was reputedly indistinguishable – Herbert, who had no wish to play against his brother. In the title match Wilfred recovered from the loss of the first two sets in beating the Australian doctor, Wilberforce Eaves, who had taken lawn tennis from England to Australia (at least at its top class level) and who ranks among the non-Wimbledon winners who deserved better. He saved a match point in the third set.

This time Wilfred reigned for just twelve months. In the Challenge round of 1896 he gave best after a very long struggle against H.S. Mahony, another of the formidable Irishmen. When he competed in 1897 Wilfred lost in the semi-finals to Reggie Doherty after beating Laurie Doherty in the round before.

In the interregnum between the Renshaws and the Dohertys the Baddeleys had done well. But Wilfred is remembered now mainly as one of the youngest champions. He was a Man of Kent.

Wimbledon Singles Record:
1890, won 2 matches, lost Willoughby Hamilton, quarter-final.
1891, won 4 matches, *champion* (sets 12–2; games 78–36).
1892, won 1 match, *champion* (sets 3–1; games 22–14).
1893, won 0 matches, lost Joshua Pim, Challenge Round.
1894, won 3 matches, lost Joshua Pim, Challenge Round.
1895, won 2 matches, *champion* (sets 6–2; games 46–34).
1896, won 0 matches, lost Harold Mahony, Challenge Round.
1897, won 2 matches, lost Reginald Doherty, semi-final.

Matches: 14–5; sets 45–20; games 339–240.

Longest Match: Challenge Round 1896, lost to Harold Mahony 2–6 8–6 7–5 6–8 3–6 – a total of 57 games.

Age on first winning singles: 19 years 174 days.

Age on last winning singles: 23 years 183 days.

Overall Record:

	Titles	Matches Played	Won	Lost
Singles	3	19	14	5
Doubles	4	21	14	7
Mixed	0	0	0	0
Total	7	40	28	12

Career Achievements:
The Championships, Wimbledon: singles 1891, 1892, 1895; doubles 1891, 1894–1896.
Irish Championships: singles 1896: doubles 1896, 1897.

Full name: Wilfred Baddeley
Born: 11th January, 1872, Bromley, Kent, England.
Died: 24th January, 1929, Mentone, France.

Joshua Pim

1893, 1894

Doctor 'X' from Bray

Joshua Pim, who was singles champion in 1893 and 1894, followed Willoby Hamilton as an Irishman who made the English look small in their own backyard. But apart from his two championships the worthy doctor, who was born in Bray, Wicklow, and qualified in Dublin, holds a piquant place in the history of the game as the only Davis Cup player whose identity was at first discreetly hidden.

The British Davis Cup team, challenging for the second time and keen to reverse the outcome of the sharp rout suffered two years earlier, was despatched by the British LTA to New York in 1902 with the anonymous Mr 'X' among its members. It was not just a ploy to have the American guessing, rather the desire to smooth some question of medical etiquette that had arisen over Pim's selection. It transpired that the home side had little to fear, for when the unknown player revealed himself at the Crescent Athletic Club as Doctor Pim, the champion of eight years before, he also revealed himself as a man who was beyond his best He lost both singles without much distinction, for his selection was rather *faute de mieux* when being a team member was a costly enterprise.

A contemporary and rival of Pim, his fellow Irishman Harold Mahony, thought so much of him that he wrote 'The general opinion of experts would seem to rank J. Pim as the finest player the world has ever seen. His game was of the very severe type, yet executed with such ease and nonchalance as to give the impression that he was taking no interest in the proceedings.'

His genius, if it were that, came into its own after being handicapped in 1891 by an injured right hand and in 1892 by a bout of typhoid. In both those years Wilfred Baddeley beat him in the title match. But in the next two years Pim beat the same man to take his two titles.

A domestic 'grand slam', if such a feat could be held to exist, was achieved by Pim in 1893. He won both the singles and the doubles (with Frank Stoker) in the three outstanding tournaments of the age, the Wimbledon, Northern and Irish Championships. His prowess stirred the mid 1890s.

Wimbledon Singles Record:
1890, won 2 matches, lost Willoughby Hamilton, semi-final.
1891, won 3 matches, lost Wilfred Baddeley, All Comers' Final.
1892, won 5 matches, lost Wilfred Baddeley, Challenge Round.
1893, won 6 matches, *champion* (sets 18–3; games 126–77).
1894, won 1 match, *champion* (sets 3–0; games 24–16).

Matches: 17–3; sets 54–20; games 434–321.

Longest Match: All Comers' Final, 1892 beat Ernest Lewis 2–6 5–7 9–7 6–3 6–2 – a total of 53 games.

Age on first winning singles: 24 years 58 days.

Age on last winning singles: 25 years 58 days.

Overall Record:

	Titles	Matches Played	Won	Lost
Singles	2	20	17	3
Doubles	2	9	7	2
Mixed	0	0	0	0
Total	4	29	24	5

Career Achievements:
The Championships, Wimbledon: singles 1893, 1894; doubles 1890, 1893.
Irish Championships: singles 1893–1895; doubles 1890, 1891, 1893–1895.
British Davis Cup team: 1902, winning 0 from 2 matches (singles 0–2) in 1 tie.

Full name: Joshua Pim
Born: 20th May, 1869, Bray, Co. Wicklow, Ireland.
Died: 12th April, 1942, Dublin, Ireland.

Harold Mahony

1896

The Last of the Irish

The Championships were staged for the 20th time in 1896 and produced the 10th men's singles champion, Harold Mahony. He was the third Irishman to win in seven years. There has not been another since. Few champions have been so popular among their rivals. His joviality was a by-word. One of them, George Hillyard, wrote 'Surely the most generous hearted, casual, irresponsible seventy-five inches of Irish bone and muscle that ever walked on court'.

He went on 'A splendid all-round player in every other respect, he could not, and never did, acquire the right method of hitting the ball on the forehand'. Yet Mahony, despite this deficiency, cavorted his happy way through the game in the mid-1890s, full of confidence, always joking with the spectators and contributing hugely to the enjoyment of the game.

He came to the fore at Wimbledon in 1891 when he reached the semi-finals of the All Comers' event only to lose to his fellow Irishman, Joshua Pim. He yielded to the same player at the same stage a year later. In 1893 he lost for the third time to Pim, this time in the All Comers' final.

He found his peak performance in 1896. On his way to the Challenge Round he beat Frank Riseley in four sets, Harold Nisbet in five and Wilberforce Eaves in three. The holder was Wilfred Baddeley, already champion three times. Their ensuing battle was the longest in number of games ever played in the title match at Worple Road. Mahony beat Baddeley 6–2 6–8 5–7 8–6 6–3. This total of 57 games was not surpassed until Jaroslav Drobny beat Ken Rosewall in 58 in 1954.

A year later Mahony gave way to Reggie Doherty; by then a new era in the game had started. Mahony was born in Scotland, though very Irish for all that. He died before his time. On the second day of The Championships in 1905, on 27th June, the lovable Mahony was found dead across his wrecked bicycle at the base of a hill in County Kerry. He was 38.

Wimbledon Singles Record:
1890, won 0 matches, lost Deane Miller, 1st round.
1891, won 3 matches, lost Joshua Pim, semi-final.
1892, won 3 matches, lost Joshua Pim, semi-final.
1893, won 4 matches, lost Joshua Pim, All Comers' Final.
1894, won 1 match, lost Ernest Lewis, 2nd round.
1895, did not play.
1896, won 6 matches, *champion* (sets 18–7; games 154–117).
1897, won 0 matches, lost Reginald Doherty, Challenge Round.
1898, won 4 matches, lost Laurence Doherty, All Comers' Final.
1899, won 3 matches, lost Arthur Gore, semi-final.
1900, won 0 matches, lost Clement Cazalet, 2nd round.
1901, won 0 matches, lost Charles Dixon, semi-final.
1902, won 3 matches, lost Laurence Doherty, semi-final.
1903, won 2 matches, lost Sidney Smith, 3rd round.
1904, won 2 matches, lost Frank Riseley, 3rd round.

Matches: 34–13; sets 113–63; games 958–792.

Longest Match: 2nd round 1900, lost Clement Cazalet 5–7 2–6 8–6 10–8 4–6 – a total of 62 games.

Age on winning singles: 29 years 158 days.

Overall Record:

	Titles	Matches Played	Won	Lost
Singles	1	47	34	13
Doubles	0	23	9	14
Mixed	0	0	0	0
Total	1	70	43	27

Career Achievements:
The Championships, Wimbledon: singles 1896.
Irish Championships: singles 1898; mixed 1895, 1896.

Full name: Harold Segerson Mahony
Born: 13th February, 1867, Edinburgh, Scotland.
Died: 27th June, 1905, in Caragh Hill, nr. Killorglin, Co. Kerry, Ireland.

Reginald Doherty

1897–1900

Delicate Genius

The champion in the four years 1897 to 1900, Reginald Doherty, was arguably the best British player of all time. He was generally held to be better than his younger brother Laurence but he was plagued all his life by ill health and died in 1910 when he was only 38. He is reputed to have declared that there was never a day when he felt really well. He was six feet one inch tall but weighed only 140 pounds.

Between them, Reggie and his younger and more robust brother transformed British lawn tennis from its decline in the mid-1890s to ever rising heights of popularity, not only by their superb skill but by their grace and charm and superb sportsmanship. In their day lawn tennis probably reached its greatest social heights, certainly in Europe, and they were regarded as princes in the *haut ton* world of the Riviera and, markedly, the imperial grandeur of the German tournaments.

The Dohertys were Londoners, their father a printer, and they lived at Clapham. But both Reggie and Laurie were born in Hartfield Road, Wimbledon, within a stone's throw of the All England Club, albeit on the other side of the London and South Western Railway. They went to Westminster and then to Cambridge. The eldest son of the family, William, went to Oxford. He, too, was a lawn tennis player and captained Oxford, but went into the church and did not play seriously. With Reggie he won the junior doubles championship of Wales.

At Westminster Reggie was a soccer player. He did not go up to Cambridge until 1894 when he was already 23 years old. He and Laurie were both in the Cambridge side that beat Oxford by 18–nil and neither ever lost a match in the Universities' contest.

Reggie was essentially a one grip player. He was a fine natural stylist with a masterly, rhythmic all court game. He had the curious habit of playing with his sleeves unrolled and unbuttoned. He claimed to be able to give 15 in handicap to his brother and win and no-one dissented. The brothers, however, disliked playing against each other.

His genius did not mature at Wimbledon until his fourth attempt in 1897 when he dispossessed Harold Mahony of Ireland without difficulty. He was without a peer for the next three years. The 1898 Challenge Round was against his brother Laurie and he won in five sets. A year later he conceded the first two sets before beating the steadiness of Arthur Gore. His fourth triumph in 1900 was against the forehand power of Sydney Smith.

In 1902 he made his mark in the US Championships at Newport. With Laurie withdrawing rather than play him in the semi-final he went on to reach the Challenge Round, losing to William Larned. The next year, when he was in the side winning the Davis Cup for the British Isles for the first time, he gave way to

Laurie when they came against each other in the quarter-final. Laurie then went on to become the first overseas winner of the US title. They won the doubles in both years.

His last appearance in The Championships was in doubles with George Simond in 1908, when they did not get far. It was a trial run of sorts for his entry soon after in the Olympics when, with George Hillyard, he won a gold medal. He was dead a little more than two years later.

Wimbledon Singles Record:
1894, won 0 matches, lost Clement Cazalet, 1st round.
1895, won 1 match, lost Herbert Baddeley, 1st round.
1896, won 0 matches, lost Harold Mahony, 1st round.
1897, won 5 matches, *champion* (sets 15–1; games 96–57).
1898, won 1 match, *champion* (sets 3–2; games 25–30)
1899, won 1 match, *champion* (sets 3–2; games 23–21).
1900, won 1 match, *champion* (sets 3–1; games 24–14).
1901, won 0 matches, lost Arthur Gore, Challenge Round.

Matches: 9–4; sets 31–19; games 254–217.

Longest Match: 1st round 1897, beat George Simond 11–9 1–6 6–4 6–3 – a total of 46 games.

Age on first winning singles: 24 years 259 days.

Age on last winning singles: 27 years 262 days.

Overall Record:

	Titles	Matches Played	Won	Lost
Singles	4	13	9	4
Doubles	8	26	21	5
Mixed	0	0	0	0
Total	12	39	30	9

Career Achievements:
The Championships, Wimbledon: singles 1897–1900; doubles 1897–1901, 1903–1905.
US Championships: doubles 1902, 1903.
Irish Championships: singles 1899–1901; doubles 1898–1902: mixed 1899, 1900.
Olympic Games: singles 1900 bronze; mixed 1900 gold; doubles 1908 gold.
British Davis Cup team: 1902–1906, winning 7 from 8 matches (singles 2–1; doubles 5–0) in 5 ties.

Full name: Reginald Frank Doherty
Born: 14th October, 1872, Wimbledon, Surrey, England.
Died: 29th December, 1910, Kensington, London, England.

Arthur Gore

1901, 1908, 1909

Everlasting Veteran

Not until the arrival of Jean Borotra in the 1920s did anyone compete in the singles for a longer period than did the enthusiastic and assiduous Arthur Gore, who was not related to Wimbledon's first champion, Spencer Gore. He first challenged in 1888. He last did so in 1922, when his age was 54, having been three times the champion, the last in 1909 when he was 41. In the doubles he went on playing until 1927. He missed the 1928 meeting and died in December that year.

Gore was certainly a late developer. He did not get beyond the third round (and as far as that only once) until a semi-final place in 1898, a decade after his first effort.

Having lost to the Irishman Harold Mahony in a five setter that year Gore became one of the more threatening competitors for the next decade and a bit. He was in the Challenge Round against Reggie Doherty in 1899 and within one match of that stage in 1900 when Sydney Smith, the Gloucestershire man with a fearsome forehand, beat him in the All Comers' final.

His first championship came in 1901 when Reggie Doherty was battling with weak health. Gore, patient and painstaking, perhaps more of a plodder than many, beat him in four sets. A year later he had to yield to Laurie Doherty, the more robust of the brothers.

In 1908 the field again opened up. There was no Norman Brookes, the Australian who had revealed his sharp and subtle genius the year before, and the New Zealander Tony Wilding was still short of his peak. Gore's crucial match was the All Comers' final against his fellow countryman Roper Barrett, who had put out Wilding. Gore, winning in the final set, took his second title at 40. He met a British challenger the following year, Major Ritchie, and Gore survived after losing the first two sets.

At the age of 42 in 1910 he could not deny the mastery of Wilding. If ever a man could have retired then with distinction it was he. Yet his enthusiasm was such that he pressed on, in singles to 1922 and in doubles to 1927. His last singles win was in 1920 when at the age of 52 he beat Gerald Sherwell 9–7 6–2 6–4 before losing to Toto Brugnon of France.

Gore, for all his success at an age when many players have given up, had his precocious side. His first tournament success was at Dinard when he was 12 years old. In contrast he is unique in being the only vice-president of the LTA to be Wimbledon singles champion at the same time!

In his penultimate championship, 1926, he had the distinction of beating the future King of England. With Roper Barrett he beat the Duke of York and Louis Greig 6–1 6–3 6–2. His last contest at Wimbledon in 1927 was a first round of the Gentlemen's doubles when with Roper Barrett he lost 3–6 6–4 6–4 12–10 to 'Skipper' Stowe (himself a leading statesman of the game some years later) and E.U. Williams.

It was 39 years since he had made his debut when he had lost in five sets to W.C. Taylor at Worple Road.

Wimbledon Singles Record:
1888, won 0 matches, lost William Taylor, 2nd round.
1889, won 0 matches, lost William Wilberforce, 1st round.
1890, won 0 matches, lost Willoby Hamilton, 1st round.
1891, won 1 match, lost Harold Mahony, 2nd round.
1892, won 2 matches, lost Harold Mahony, quarter-final.
1893, won 1 match, lost Harry Barlow, 2nd round.
1894, won 0 matches, lost Ernest Lewis, 1st round.
1895, did not play.
1896, won 0 matches, lost Wilberforce Eaves, 1st round (won plate).
1897, won 1 match, lost George Greville, 2nd round
1898, won 3 matches, lost Harold Mahony, semi-final.
1899, won 5 matches, lost Reginald Doherty, Challenge Round.
1900, won 4 matches, lost Sidney Smith, All Comers' Final.
1901, won 6 matches, *champion* (sets 18–5; games 130–88).
1902, won 0 matches, lost Laurence Doherty, Challenge Round.
1903, won 1 match, lost Sidney Smith, 2nd round (won plate).
1904, won 2 matches, lost Frank Riseley, quarter-final.
1905, won 4 matches, lost Norman Brookes, semi-final.
1906, won 5 matches, lost Frank Riseley, All Comers' Final.

1907, won 5 matches, lost Norman Brookes, All Comers' Final.
1908, won 6 matches, *champion* (sets 18–3; games 131–80).
1909, won 1 match, *champion* (sets 3–2; games 25–20).
1910, won 0 matches, lost Anthony Wilding, Challenge Round.
1911, won 3 matches, lost Max Decugis, 4th round.
1912, won 6 matches, lost Anthony Wilding, Challenge Round.
1913, won 3 matches, lost Oskar Kreuzer, 4th round.
1914, won 4 matches, lost Norman Brookes, quarter-final.
1919, won 0 matches, lost Frank Jarvis, 1st round.
1920, won 1 match, lost Jacques Brugnon, 2nd round.
1921, won 0 matches, lost Sydney Jacobs, 1st round.
1922, won 0 matches, lost Ali-Hassen Fyzee, 1st round.

Matches: 64–26; sets 216–109; games 1711–1342.

Longest Match: 1st round 1891, beat Herbert Baddeley 5–7 10–8 6–4 4–6 6–2 – a total of 58 games.

Age on first winning singles: 33 years 180 days.

Age on last winning singles: 41 years 182 days.

Overall Record:

	Titles	Matches Played	Won	Lost
Singles	3	90	64	26
Doubles	1	60	33	27
Mixed	0	5	2	3
Total	4	155	99	56

Career Achievement
The Championships, Wimbledon: singles 1901, 1908, 1909; doubles 1909.
Olympic Games: singles (Covered) 1908 gold, doubles (Covered) 1908 gold.
British Davis Cup team: 1900, 1907, 1912, winning 3 from 7 matches (singles 2–3 1 unf; doubles 1–0) in 3 ties.

Full name: Arthur William (Wentworth) Charles Gore
Born: 2nd January, 1868, Lyndhurst, Hampshire, England.
Died: 1st December, 1928, Kensington, London, England.

Laurence Doherty

1902–1906

Perfect Sportsman

When Laurence Doherty died, aged only 43, in 1919 it was 13 years since he was Wimbledon champion. More than a decade had passed since his greatness had captivated the world. Nonetheless *The Times* was constrained to publish a leader about his passing. It stressed his greatness as a player but went on:

> 'With him there was no possibility of 'unpleasant incidents'; he was too true a sportsman to commit an ungenerous act deliberately, too cool to seize in the excitement of the moment an advantage he might subsequently regret. Defeat at his hands lost half its sting, for he was courtesy itself; and if defeat was his own portion he accepted it with the same equanimity which had made it so difficult to bring about. He played

an English game in the spirit in which Englishmen think games should be played. He was a typical Englishman, and it is a source of legitimate pride to his countrymen that we can call him so.'

The chauvinism may be forgiven in the aftermath of the First World War. The tribute underlines the appeal and charisma Laurie Doherty had possessed. His predecessor in the line of heroic champions was William Renshaw, his successor the New Zealander Tony Wilding. Later there was Britain's Fred Perry, more recently Bjorn Borg, Pete Sampras and Roger Federer.

Three years younger than Reggie he followed his brother to Westminster and to Trinity Hall, Cambridge. He was the more robust by far, though at Westminster whereas Reggie had been a soccer player, he had been a sprinter. Their relative skills as lawn tennis players could be debated. Contemporaries held that Reggie was the better but they disliked playing one another. Certainly Laurie built the better of the two great records of achievement in the game.

Having been North of England junior champion at Scarborough at the age of 15 in 1890 he went up to Cambridge in 1896, only two years after his brother, despite the three years between them.

He competed at Wimbledon for the first time that year. Curiously he was beaten in his debut match in the first round by Clement Cazalet, the man who had also beaten Reggie in his first match two years earlier.

Whereas Reggie had won the Wimbledon singles at his fourth attempt Laurie was competing for the seventh time when he won in 1902. He had come near in 1898 when he reached the Challenge Round only to lose over five sets to his brother. He was 26. Reggie had been 22 when he first won.

Laurie did not have Reggie in contention in 1902 and his fluent mastery was seriously disputed only in a semi-final against the subtle, volatile and gentle craft of Ireland's Harold Mahony, the champion in the last year before the Doherty era. Mahony won the first two sets but ran himself into utter exhaustion in doing so and had to retire in the fourth.

Over the next four years Laurie controlled The Championships. In three of the challenge rounds he beat Frank Riseley and only once lost a set. In the penultimate year, 1905, he was challenged by the novice Australian Norman Brookes, destined to be the first overseas winner of the Gentlemen's singles two years later, and lost no set. He was again unbeaten in 1907. In doubles he and Reggie came near to complete invincibility. Having first won in 1897 they won seven more titles together, losing but twice, in 1902 to Riseley and Smith and to the same pair in 1906.

Laurie was as good in the United States as at home and also excellent on the slow courts of the fashionable tournaments of the Riviera and Germany. He conceded a walk-over to Reggie when they might have met in the US Nationals in 1902. In 1903 he was given the same courtesy and went through to win the title, the first overseas man to do so. The brothers won the doubles both years. In the Davis Cup Laurie was impeccable. He contested seven singles and five doubles and won the lot, all in the Challenge Round. In the Olympics of 1900, played in Paris, he won gold in singles and doubles. He had an interesting partnership in the mixed, with Marion Jones, the first American woman to compete at Wimbledon. They won a bronze medal.

Laurence Doherty lives in the history of the game as the perfect gentleman and, in the eyes of his contemporaries, the perfect player. He became a good golfer.

Unlike Reggie he changed his grip between forehand and backhand. Overhead he reputedly never failed to kill the ball from any part of the court.

In the First World War he was invalided out of the Anti-Aircraft branch of the RNR. He died after a long illness.

Wimbledon Singles Record:

1896, won 0 matches, lost Clement Cazalet, first round.
1897, won 2 matches, lost Wilfred Baddeley, quarter final.
1898, won 5 matches, lost Reginald Doherty, Challenge Round.
1899, did not play.
1900, won 3 matches, lost Arthur Gore, semi-final.
1901, won 1 match, lost George Hillyard, 3rd round.
1902, won 5 matches, *champion* (sets 14–4; games 101–68).
1903, won 1 match, *champion* (sets 3–0; games 19–8).
1904, won 1 match, *champion* (sets 3–0; games 21–12).
1905, won 1 match, *champion* (sets 3–0; games 20–12).
1906, won 1 match, *champion* (sets 3–1; games 22–15).

Matches: 20–5; sets 65–23; games 487–329.

Longest Match: All Comers' Final 1898, beat Harold Mahony 6–1 6–2 4–6 2–6 14–12 – a total of 59 games.

Age on first winning singles: 26 years 265 days.

Age on last winning singles: 30 years 269 days.

Overall Record:

	Titles	Matches Played	Won	Lost
Singles	5	25	20	5
Doubles	8	22	18	4
Mixed	0	0	0	0
Total	13	47	38	9

Career Achievements:

The Championships, Wimbledon: singles 1902–1906; doubles 1897–1901, 1903, 1904, 1905.
US Championships: singles 1903; doubles 1902, 1903.
Irish Championships: singles 1902; doubles 1898–1902; mixed 1901, 1902.
Olympic Games: singles 1900 gold; doubles 1900 gold; mixed 1900 bronze.
British Davis Cup team: 1902–1906, unbeaten in 7 singles, 5 doubles, in 5 ties.

Full name: Hugh Laurence Doherty
Born: 8th October, 1875, Wimbledon, Surrey, England.
Died: 21st August, 1919, Broadstairs, Kent, England.

Norman Brookes

1907, 1914

The Australian Master

Norman Brookes, who was from Melbourne, was the first man from overseas, the first left-hander and the first Australian to win the singles. Among men he was the forerunner of the international field that has increasingly dominated The Championships since his time.

He first challenged in 1905 and made his mark by reaching the Challenge Round. That was after a tremendous five set struggle in the All Comers' Final against the trenchant forehand of Sydney Smith. Then he met Laurie Doherty at his peak. He made five visits in all and only in 1924, when he was 46, did he fail at any stage prior to the exalted title match.

His style was unorthodox, not only for left-handedness. He played his backhand with the same racket face as his forehand. The dexterity of his angled volleying was legendary.

The last three rounds in 1907 were the easier for Brookes and he lost no set. Laurie Doherty was not defending and the All Comers' Final, which was against Arthur Gore, was the vital contest. But in round two Brookes had a hard five setter against his Australasian Davis Cup colleague, Tony Wilding, and in round four the American Karl Behr was a threat over the same distance.

Brookes was unable to return to Wimbledon until 1914. He began by winning 6–0 6–0 6–0, a very rare score among the men, and since he lost only two games in the second round and three in the third he arrived in the quarter-finals having lost a total of only five games. But he was under the hottest pressure in the All Comers'

Final from the German Otto Froitzheim and won only by 8–6 in the fifth set in the 51st game. In the Challenge Round he dispossessed his Davis Cup team mate Wilding, robbing him of what would have been his fifth title.

Sportingly Brookes came back in 1919 to defend his title, despite being 41. A powerful Australian came through against him, Gerald Patterson, who was far too paceful. He was a less serious contender at his last appearance in 1924 but nonetheless he came through three rounds before losing to Jean Washer of Belgium.

His Davis Cup achievements were high. He was five times on the winning Australasian side, playing both singles and doubles save for his appearance in doubles only in the 1919 team. When he turned out for his last tie in 1920, when the USA beat Australasia in New Zealand, he was 43.

Brookes was also a first class golfer and cricketer. Outside the sporting world he was probably the most distinguished of all Wimbledon champions and was one of the leading personalities of Australia. He was dubbed Sir Norman Brookes in 1939. He died in 1968 in his 91st year.

Wimbledon Singles Record:
1905, won 7 matches, lost Laurence Doherty, Challenge Round.
1906, did not play.
1907, won 7 matches, *champion* (sets 21–4; games 137–66)
1908–1913 did not play.
1914, won 7 matches, *champion* (sets 21–2; games 139–53).
1919, won 0 matches, lost Gerald Patterson, Challenge Round.
1920–1923 did not play.
1924, won 3 matches, lost Jean Washer, 4th Round.

Matches: 24–3; sets 72–20; games 505–287.

Longest Match: All Comers' Final 1914, beat Otto Froitzheim 6–2 6–1 5–7 4–6 8–6 – a total of 51 games.

Age on first winning singles: 29 years 232 days.

Age on last winning singles: 36 years 232 days.

Overall Record:

	Titles	Matches		
		Played	Won	Lost
Singles	2	27	24	3
Doubles	2	28	24	4
Mixed	0	0	0	0
Total	4	55	48	7

Career Achievements:
The Championships, Wimbledon: singles 1907, 1914; doubles 1907, 1914.
US Championships: doubles 1919.
Australian Championships: singles 1911; doubles 1924.
Australasian Davis Cup team: 1905, 1907–1909, 1911, 1912, 1914, 1919, 1920, winning 28 from 39 matches (singles 18–7; doubles 10–4) in 14 ties.

Full name: (Sir) Norman Everard Brookes
Born: 14th November, 1877, Melbourne, Australia.
Died: 28th September, 1968, Melbourne, Australia.

Anthony Wilding

1910–1913

Pre War Idol

The frenzied crowd scenes at Wimbledon in the 1970s, when Ilie Nastase and Bjorn Borg, idols of teen-age enthusiasts, had to be escorted by police on their way to court, would not have surprised the champion in the years just before the First World War. In the more discrete manner of the early twentieth century the New Zealander Tony Wilding became an idol of spectators everywhere.

He was everything an idealised hero of the time should be. He was handsome, he was well mannered and his physical prowess was of the highest order. At lawn tennis he excelled, with a beauty and fluency of style but he was also very much of the modern age. He was a sporting motorist, both with cars and with motor cycles. He learned to fly. And he was very much a gentleman by the standards of the time, having been at Cambridge and qualified as a barrister.

He came from Christchurch but after Cambridge he made England more or less his home. Between 1904 and the outbreak of war he failed to play only at the 1909 meeting. In taking his first singles the following year his crucial match was the All Comers' Final against the American Beals Wright. Wilding won after losing the first two sets. It was easier in the subsequent Challenge Round against Arthur Gore.

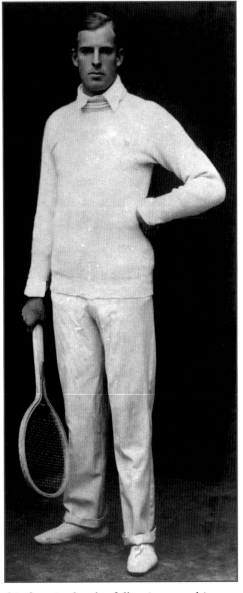

His defence in 1911 was fraught. His challenger, the wily Roper Barrett, set out to soft ball and lob him into ineptitude and, on a baking day, all but succeeded. The fitter Wilding shook himself out of his trance when trailing two sets to one. He took the fourth set so convincingly that the exhausted Barrett retired. A year later he took his third title by again beating Gore.

His fourth title match, against Maurice McLoughlin, the Califomian, was his most famous. McLoughlin had astonished Europe by his cannon ball service and he was reckoned powerful enough to conquer all. As far as the Challenge Round he did so impressively. At that stage Wilding, a New Zealander, found himself in the position of defending the honour of the European game *vis-à-vis* America. He was good enough to turn the pace of McLoughlin against its perpetrator, all in three sets.

It is significant, perhaps, that in both the years Norman Brookes won the singles he beat his doubles partner, Wilding, in doing so. In 1907 it was in the second round. In 1914 it was in the Challenge Round and Wilding was denied his fifth championship. A gifted pupil submitted to his master.

Wilding and Brookes were the mainstay of what was then Australasian Davis Cup strength. Just the two of them won the trophy in 1907, 1908, 1909 and 1914.

Wilding never played in the US Championships. He entered in 1914, for he was in the Australasian side that won the Davis Cup from the USA at Forest Hills. By then World War I had started and Wilding did not go on to Newport. Rather he returned to Europe to enlist.

He joined the Royal Marines. By October he was on the Western Front. He was killed by shell fire at Neuve Chapelle on May 9th 1915. He had long been a sporting hero and he died a war hero. New Zealand never had a greater player.

Wimbledon Singles Record:
1904, won 1 match, lost Harold Mahony, 2nd round.
1905, won 3 matches, lost Arthur Gore, quarter-final.
1906, won 4 matches, lost Arthur Gore, semi-final.
1907, won 1 match, lost Norman Brookes, 2nd round (won plate).
1908, won 3 matches, lost Herbert Barrett, quarter-final.
1909, did not play.
1910, won 8 matches, *champion* (sets 24–5; games 167–77).
1911, won 1 match *champion* (sets 2–2; games 18–18).
1912, won 1 match, *champion* (sets 3–1; games 22–18).
1913, won 1 match, *champion* (sets 3–0; games 24–17).
1914, won 0 matches, lost Norman Brookes, Challenge Round.

Matches: 23–6; sets 72–32; games 568–398.

Longest Match: 4th round 1905 beat William Clothier 5–7 1–6 8–8 7–5 10–8 – a total of 63 games.

Age on first winning singles: 26 years 242 days.

Age on last winning singles: 29 years 246 days.

Overall Record:

	Titles	Matches Played	Won	Lost
Singles	4	29	23	6
Doubles	4	39	33	6
Mixed	0	6	5	1
Total	8	74	61	13

Career Achievements:

The Championships, Wimbledon: singles 1910–1913; doubles 1907, 1908, 1910, 1914.
Australian Championships: singles 1906, 1909; doubles 1906.
Australasian Davis Cup team: 1905–1909, 1914 winning 21 from 30 matches (singles 15–6; doubles 6–3) in 11 ties.

Full name: Anthony Frederick Wilding
Born: 31st October, 1883, Christchurch, New Zealand.
Died: 9th May, 1915, Neuve Chapelle, France.

Gerald Patterson

1919, 1922

Australian Power House

In the aftermath of the war in 1919 Gerald Patterson, who had won an M.C. in that conflict, arrived from Melbourne like an Australian in a hurry. He was strong and his service was overwhelmingly fast, with a second delivery that was nearly as good as the first. He was an effective pace maker all round. His backhand was vulnerable, though only very good players could exploit that relative weakness.

Patterson had the distinction not only of winning the singles at his first attempt but in being the first man to win eight matches to do so. It took him seven rounds to win the All Comers' and the eighth was the Challenge Round, this against his fellow Australian Norman Brookes.

He was only once taken beyond three sets, by Britain's astute Major Ritchie in the semi-final. He was a complete and impressive victor all through. When he defended in 1920 the American Tilden (another first time winner and survivor also of eight rounds) was too astute for his pace making.

Patterson came back in 1922 when The Championships moved to Church Road and the challenge round system abolished. This time he was invincible in six rounds after a first round walkover. He was hard pressed in the fourth round by Britain's Algernon Kingscote and by his compatriot James Anderson in the semi-finals. He trailed one set to two against both. In the final he beat Randolph Lycett in four sets. Lycett was British but had played much in Australia and, indeed, had before the war turned down a chance to play for that nation in the Davis Cup.

Patterson played only once more at Wimbledon, in 1928, when he was in Europe as the Australian Davis Cup captain. He was then 32 but won a 76 games

battle against Charles Kingsley before losing to Toto Brugnon of France in the fourth round.

Like Brookes, Patterson was a rich and distinguished public figure in Australia quite apart from his lawn tennis fame. He was a nephew of the singer Dame Nellie Melba.

Wimbledon Singles Record:
1919, won 8 matches, *champion* (sets 24–1; games 154–72).
1920, won 0 matches, lost William Tilden, Challenge Round.
1921, did not play.
1922, won 6 matches, *champion* (sets 18–5; games 133–78).
1923–1927,did not play.
1928, seeded 8, won 3 matches lost Jacques Brugnon, 4th round.

Matches: 17–2; sets 53–15; games 399–248.

Longest Match: 3rd round 1928, beat Charles Kingsley 10–8 9–11 10–8 5–7 6–2 – a total of 76 games.

Age on first winning singles: 23 years 202 days.

Age on last winning singles: 26 years 205 days.

Overall Record:

	Titles	Matches Played	Won	Lost
Singles	2	19	17	2
Doubles	0	17	14	3
Mixed	1	6	6	0
Total	3	42	37	5

Career Achievements:
The Championships, Wimbledon: singles 1919, 1922; mixed 1920.
US Championships: doubles 1919.
Australian Championships: singles 1927; doubles 1914, 1922, 1925, 1926, 1927.
Total Grand Slam titles: 10 – singles 3, doubles 6, mixed 1.
Australasian/Australian Davis Cup team: 1919, 1920, 1922, 1924, 1925, 1928, winning 32 from 46 matches (singles 21–10; doubles 11–4) in 16 ties.

Full name: Gerald Leighton Patterson
Born: 17 December, 1895, Melbourne, Australia.
Died: 13 June, 1967, Melbourne, Australia.

Bill Tilden

1920, 1921, 1930

Long Lived Greatness

Many have claimed that 'Big Bill' Tilden, as he was known in contrast to his US rival 'Little Bill' Johnston, was the greatest player of all time. He won the Wimbledon title three times but his more impressive record was in the United States, where he played through and won the singles six years in succession and seven times in all. Equally impressive was his Davis Cup record. In seven years he won 13 successive singles in the Challenge Round.

Tilden's first major triumph at Wimbledon was in winning eight matches and easily beating the Australian Gerald Patterson in the Challenge Round. His successful defence in 1921, the last year in which the challenge round system was used and the last of the championships at the original All England Club in Worple Road, was after a still puzzling match against the challenging Brian Norton of South Africa. He lost the first two sets and in the fifth was twice match point down at 4–5 before winning 4–6 2–6 6–1 6–0 7–5.

Tilden was already 27 when he won at Wimbledon in 1920. He did not return after 1921 until 1927. That was the year when the Frenchman Henri Cochet had his heroic success and not the least of the extraordinary recoveries he made was his semi-final against Tilden. The American, two sets in front, was within sight of victory when he led 5–1 in the third set. But from 15 all Tilden lost the next 17 points in a row and was beaten 2–6 4–6 7–5 6–4 6–3.

He failed again in 1928, again in the semi-finals, but this time to another Frenchman, Rene Lacoste. Then in 1929 he fell again to Cochet, once more in the semi-finals. So when he came back in 1930, after three successive failures and now 37 years old, his chances did not appear good. Again he met a Frenchman in the semi-finals, Jean Borotra. Tilden cleared this hurdle by the dramatic score of 0–6 6–4 4–6 6–0 7–5 and beat his compatriot Wilmer Allison in the final.

It was his farewell to The Championships. He first came in glory in 1920 and he left in glory 10 years later.

With a cannon ball service and a rich all round game, with a complete mastery of tactics, Tilden laid claim as the greatest ever. At Wimbledon he won three times in six attempts and never lost before the semifinals.

'Big Bill' was not inordinately tall. His height was 6 feet one inch. The zenith of Tilden's match winning career may be measured from the Wimbledon meeting in 1920 to February 1926. During that invincible

period he became Wimbledon Champion twice, US Champion six times, World Hard Court Champion in Paris, and won his singles in seven Davis Cup ties. His major victims included Gerald Patterson (with five wins), William Johnston his great American rival (whom he beat five times also in major clashes), Norman Brookes, Jean Borotra and Rene Lacoste. This impeccable spell ended when in an indoor international against France in New York he lost 11–13 3–6 to Borotra.

His world ranking was number one for six successive years from 1920 to 1925.

Outside the glory of his lawn tennis career Tilden, who was a member of a distinguished Philadelphia family, had a life containing much frustration. He had more intellectual aspirations than most players but failed in his attempts both to be an actor and a playwright. He was in dispute with the US ruling body over his status as an amateur at a time when 'shamateurism' existed and was liable to disciplinary sanction.

He turned professional in December 1930 and took the professional game to new frontiers. He remained a top line player for many years and was still active when he died in Los Angeles in 1953 at the age of 60. But the greatest frustration of his life must have been his covert homosexuality. He did not live long enough to see that trait taken out of the shadows. Tilden may be claimed as the greatest player in the game. He could also be said to have been one of the most tragic.

Wimbledon Singles Record:

1920, won 8 matches, *champion* (sets 24–2; games 171–107).
1921, won 1 match, *champion* (sets 3–2; games 25–18).
1922–1926, did not play.
1927, seeded 2, won 5 matches, lost Henri Cochet, semi-final.
1928, seeded 3 won 5 matches, lost Rene Lacoste, semi-final.
1929, seeded 3, won 5 matches lost Henri Cochet, semi-final.
1930, seeded 2, won 7 matches *champion* (sets 21–2; games 135–69).

Matches: 31–3; sets 97–22; games 680–392.

Longest Match: 4th round 1920, beat Algernon Kingscote 6–3 5–7 6–4 5–7 6–3 – a total of 52 games.

Age on first winning singles: 27 years 144 days.

Age on last winning singles: 37 years 145 days.

Overall Record:

	Titles	Matches Played	Won	Lost
Singles	3	34	31	3
Doubles	1	25	21	4
Mixed	0	9	6	3
Total	4	68	58	10

Career Achievements:

The Championships, Wimbledon: singles 1920, 1921, 1930; doubles 1927.
US Championships: singles 1920, 1921, 1922, 1923, 1924, 1925, 1929; doubles 1918, 1921, 1922, 1923, 1927; mixed 1913, 1914, 1922, 1923.
French Championships: mixed 1930.
Total Grand Slam titles: 21 – singles 10, doubles 6, mixed 5.
Italian Championships: singles 1930; doubles 1930.
US Davis Cup team: 1920–1930, winning 34 from 41 matches (singles 25–5; doubles 9–2) in 17 ties.

Full name: William Tatem Tilden
Born: 10th February 1893, Germantown, Pennsylvania, USA.
Died: 5th June, 1953, Los Angeles, California, USA.

William Johnston

1923

In the Shadow of Tilden

He was called 'Little Bill' Johnston in contrast to 'Big Bill' Tilden who was nearly two years his senior and much taller. He was the second Californian – the first was Maurice McLoughlin – to take the fame of that state into the international lawn tennis arena. But no man could have been in greater contrast to the hard hitting McLoughlin. Johnston was not only diminutive but a classicist in his style, with fluency and strength of ground stroke his major forte.

Originally he was well ahead of Tilden. He won his first US Singles title in 1915 and beat Tilden to win the final in 1919. He came with Tilden to Wimbledon in 1920 and that meeting marked the transition of Tilden to invincibility. Johnston spent the rest of his career in Tilden's shadow.

Every year from 1920 to 1925 Johnston hauled himself to within one match of winning back the US National singles title. In every one of those years Tilden thwarted him. The dominance of both came to an end in 1926 when the rising strength of the great Frenchmen, Jean Borotra, Rene Lacoste and Henri Cochet was fulfilled.

He competed only twice at Wimbledon, losing to the Irishman James Parke in 1920 in the 2nd round over four sets and 42 much praised games. Tilden was not with him when he came back in 1923

when he was outstanding. The only set he lost was in the quarter-finals against Hon. Cecil Campbell, an Irishman like Parke.

His was the first all–American singles final, against Frank Hunter who won only four games. The same year he won the World Hard Court men's singles title in Paris and was accordingly 'World Champion' on both Hard and Grass Courts in the last year those grandiose titles pertained.

Wimbledon Singles Record:
1920, won 1 match, lost James Parke, 2nd round.
1921, 1922, did not play.
1923, won 7 matches, *champion* (sets 21–1; games 135–60).

Matches: 8–1; sets 25–4; games 172–91.

Longest Match: 2nd round 1920, lost James Parke 5–7 6–2 2–6 6–8 – a total of 42 games.

Age on winning singles: 28 years 247 days.

Overall Record:

	Titles	Matches Played	Won	Lost
Singles	1	9	8	1
Doubles	0	5	4	1
Mixed	0	2	1	1
Total	1	16	13	3

Career Achievements:
The Championships, Wimbledon: singles 1923.
US Championships: singles 1915, 1919; doubles 1915, 1916, 1920; mixed 1921.
Total Grand Slam titles: 7 – singles 3, doubles 3, mixed 1.
World Hard Court Championships: singles 1923.
US Davis Cup team: 1920–1927, winning 18 from 21 matches (singles 14–3; doubles 4–0) in 10 ties.

Full name: William Johnston
Born: 2nd November, 1894, San Francisco, California, USA.
Died: 1st May, 1946, San Francisco, California, USA.

Jean Borotra

1924, 1926

Everlasting Zest

The long-lasting enthusiasm of Jean Borotra is unequalled in the annals of Wimbledon, surpassing even that of Arthur Gore, who played first in 1888 and 39 years later in 1927. Borotra competed first in 1922 and last in 1964, a spell of 42 years – and to extend his zeal further he went on competing in the veteran's events until 1977, no less than 55 years after his debut. He is unique in having played at Wimbledon in all the anniversary celebrations, the 50th, the 75th and the 100th!

Borotra was popularly known as the 'Bounding Basque' and, in British eyes, the favourite among the 'Four Musketeers' who dominated the game so richly in the Golden Age of the 1920s and 1930s. He was indeed a proud Basque and his acrobatic volleying gave him his sobriquet. He was the apostle of the serve and volley game, a tactic he carried to the extreme. It meant his going all out for a set, then resting to recuperate his energies.

Prior to 1939 he captivated Wimbledon crowds more than any player before him. He had only to don his black beret at the change of ends, this being the signal for a major effort, to bring the Centre Court crowd applauding wildly. That he used his popularity to his own advantage was obvious. He was less popular as an opponent. He was a great, if sometimes volatile, match player. From the start of his career to the end he engaged in a running battle with the foot fault judge. He was good theatre, if one may use that term in relation to sport, to the nth degree.

He was decorated in the First World War. In the second he became the Minister of Sport in the Vichy Government. This brought eventual imprisonment by the Gestapo in their VIP camp. It also brought post war difficulties when the Wimbledon authorities, taking their cue from a 'black list' compiled by the Foreign Office, refused his Wimbledon entry in 1946. This all blew over but it marred the continuity of Borotra's passion for playing.

He won the singles at his third attempt, beating his Davis Cup team mate René Lacoste in a five set final. The following year he lost to the same player at the same stage, yielding in four sets. He had an American opponent in his next winning final in 1926, beating Howard Kinsey in three sets. This was the only time in six continuous years the singles final was not all French.

He was denied his third title in 1927 when he was involved in the last of Henri Cochet's hair-raising victories. He was six times at match point against Cochet – and on one of the six he drew the attention of the umpire to the fact that the ball, before falling out, had touched him – before that miracle man won 4–6 4–6 6–3 6–4 7–5.

His fifth final in six years was in 1929 when he lost again to Cochet, albeit more easily. He played his last singles in 1935 and retired from the singles game, claiming he was too old.

His complete statistics are recorded below and refer to his

Championships record. As a veteran he can be credited with two wins and 15 losses in the men's doubles. His final Championship totals: matches Won 154; Lost 69, total 223.

He excelled on wood courts. He won the British Covered Courts singles 11 times between 1926 and 1949 and the same French title 12 times between 1922 and 1947. He was also a four times winner of the US Indoor singles 1925 to 1931.

Wimbledon Singles Record:
1922, won 2 matches, lost Gerald Patterson, 3rd round.
1923, won 3 matches, lost Brian Norton, 4th round.
1924, won 7 matches, *champion* (sets 21–6; games 160–109).
1925, won 6 matches, lost Rene Lacoste, final.
1926, won 7 matches, *champion* (sets 21–5; games 149–111).
1927, seeded 3, won 6 matches, lost Henri Cochet, final.
1928, seeded 5, won 4 matches, lost William Tilden, quarter-final.

1929, seeded 2 won 6 matches, lost Henri Cochet, final.
1930, seeded 3, won 5 matches, lost William Tilden, semi-final.
1931, seeded 1, won 5 matches, lost Frank Shields, semi-final.
1932, seeded 7, won 3 matches, lost Enrique Maier, 4th round.
1933, 1934, did not play singles.
1935, unseeded, won 1 match, lost Roderick Menzel, 2nd round.

Matches: 55–10; sets 175–72; games 1360–1044.

Longest Match: 2nd round 1925, beat Noel Turnbull 10–8 5–7 7–5 10–8 – a total of 60 games.

Age on first winning singles: 25 years 327 days.

Age on last winning singles: 27 years 323 days.

Overall Record:

	Titles	Matches Played	Won	Lost
Singles	2	65	55	10
Doubles	3	90	59	31
Mixed	1	68	40	28
Total	6	223	154	69

Career Achievements:
The Championships, Wimbledon: singles 1924, 1926; doubles 1925, 1932, 1933; mixed 1925.
US Championships: mixed 1926.
French Championships: singles 1931; doubles 1925, 1928, 1929, 1934, 1936; mixed 1927, 1934.
Australian Championships: singles 1928; doubles 1928; mixed 1928.
Total Grand Slam titles: 15 – singles 3, doubles 8, mixed 4.
Olympic Games: doubles 1924 bronze.
French Davis Cup team: 1922–1937, winning 36 from 54 matches (singles 19–12; doubles 17–6) in 32 ties.

Full name: Jean Robert Borotra
Born: 13th August, 1898, Arbonne, Basses-Pyrenees, France.
Died: 17th July, 1994, Arbonne, Basses-Pyrenees, France.

Rene Lacoste

1925, 1928

Planned Precision

Any coach anxious to learn the strengths, subtleties and techniques of the leading players in the late 1920s could do no better than obtain the notebooks maintained by Rene Lacoste in his heyday as a champion. This outstanding Frenchman was the solid, sober member of the 'Four Musketeers' with Jean Borotra, Henri Cochet and Toto Brugnon. He was a thinker, not an inspirationalist. He studied his opponents and he planned his matches. His acute tactical sense was worked out in precise accuracy of driving. That he should have excelled on rubble courts was not surprising. That he should have excelled also on the fast grass of Wimbledon and, even more, on the unpredictable turf in the USA was remarkable.

Lacoste's debut at Wimbledon, in 1922, was in the first tournament at the new site of the All England Club in Church Road. He was not quite 18 and on the very damp grass of that year he lost in the first round to the Australian Pat O'Hara Wood. He was routed and won only four games in all. In the next two years, when his game matured, he throve increasing, winning three matches in 1923. In 1924, having survived a second round contest of 61 games against Manuel Alonso of Spain, he reached the final where he yielded to Borotra in five sets.

The first of his two successes at The Championships came in 1925. He was never taken beyond four sets and he avenged himself in the final against Borotra. Earlier he had won the first of his three French Championships in the initial year of its status as an international meeting. In the United States he and Borotra took France to their first of its Challenge Round in the Davis Cup. Notably in a dead match Tilden lost the first two sets before beating him in 65 games. Their acute rivalry was a high point of the game in the next few years.

Lacoste was ill and did not defend his Wimbledon title in 1926. His 'delicate' health was to bring retirement at the height of his career. Later that year he won the first of his successive victories in the US Nationals, the first overseas victor since Britain's Laurie Doherty more than two decades before. Again in the Davis Cup Challenge Round he met Tilden in a dead match. This time he won in four sets.

In 1927 Lacoste was thwarted by Borotra in the semi-finals at Wimbledon. Elsewhere his triumphs were huge. He beat Tilden (by 11–9 in the fifth set) to win the French Championship. He beat the same man to win the US title. And in the Davis Cup his win over Tilden in the fourth match, when the US were leading two matches to one, projected France towards their first victory.

Lacoste made regal progress at the 1928 Wimbledon. In his last two rounds he beat Borotra and Cochet. He was only just 24. It was his last year. After taking the French title in 1929 he gave in to poor health. He played his last singles in beating Borotra in the French singles final. He played his last serious match when he partnered Borotra to take the men's doubles.

He knew precisely what he could do on court. He also knew what his opponents could do and thwarted them. He was the last of the great players to win from the back of the court until the arrival of Bjorn Borg in the 1970s.

Wimbledon Singles Record:
1922, won 0 matches, lost Pat Wood, 1st round.
1923, won 3 matches, lost Cecil Campbell, 5th round.
1924, won 6 matches, lost Jean Borotra, final.
1925, won 7 matches, *champion* (sets 21–3; games 147–91).
1926, did not play.
1927, seeded 1, won 5 matches, lost Jean Borotra, semi-final.
1928, seeded 2, won 7 matches, *champion* (sets 21–7; games 154–107).

Matches: 28–4; sets 90–28; games 647–426.

Longest Match: 2nd round 1924, beat Manuel Alonso 2–6 6–2 13–15 6–3 6–2 – a total of 61 games.

Age on first winning singles: 21 years 2 days.

Age on last winning singles: 24 years 4 days.

Overall Record:

	Titles	Matches Played	Won	Lost
Singles	2	32	28	4
Doubles	1	18	14	4
Mixed	0	2	1	1
Total	3	52	43	9

Career Achievements:
The Championships, Wimbledon: singles 1925, 1928; doubles 1925.
US Championships: singles 1926, 1927.
French Championships: singles 1925, 1927, 1929; doubles 1925, 1929.
Total Grand Slam titles: 10 – singles 7, doubles 3.
Olympic Games: doubles 1924 bronze.
French Davis Cup team: 1923–1928, winning 40 from 51 matches (singles 32–8; doubles 8–3) in 26 ties.

Full name: Jean Rene Lacoste
Born: 2nd July, 1904, Paris, France.
Died: 12th October, 1996, St. Jean de Luz, France.

Henri Cochet

1927, 1929

Genius Extraordinary

Henri Cochet, one of the 'Four Musketeers' whose exploits gilded the later 1920s, came, like the irrepressible Jean Borotra and the studious Rene Lacoste, as a new boy to the inaugural year of Wimbledon at Church Road in 1922. His unorthodox play made its mark. In his first match he came back after losing the first two sets to beat William Crawley, who had been one of the leading British players. Such adventures became his hallmark. He seemed never to hit the ball normally if it were possible to half volley. He seemed never to hurry on the court and gave the air of being disinterested.

He challenged next in 1925. In the quarter-finals he again rallied from a two sets to love deficit, against the American John Hennessey. His team mate Borotra beat him in the semi-finals. He also lost to Borotra at the same stage in 1926, by which stage five of his 13 winning singles had been over five sets.

In 1927 Cochet won his first championship in a manner not equalled before or since. In the quarter-finals he won 3–6 3–6 6–2 6–2 6–3 against the American Frank Hunter, by 2–6 4–6 7–5 6–4 6–3 in the semi-finals against Tilden (who led 5–1 in the third set and lost 17 points in a row from 15 all in the seventh game) and then by 4–6 4–6 6–3 6–4 7–5 in the final against Borotra, who had six match points. Could any champion have won more dangerously?

He lost in the final to Lacoste in 1928 and did not go beyond four sets in any match. In 1929 he had just one five setter, in the third round against the Ireland's Lyttleton Rogers, before winning the last four rounds in three sets, the last two against Tilden and Borotra.

As a two-fold champion he had adventures still. In 1930 he won two five setters in the course of reaching the quarter-finals where he lost to the American Wilmer Allison. In 1931 he was seeded second and lost in the first round to

Britain's Nigel Sharpe. Seeded top in 1932 he fell in the second round to Ian Collins and went on to win the consolation plate.

He played for the last time in 1933 when his genius flowered more brightly. After a five setter in the third round he gave best to the hard hitting of Ellsworth Vines, then defending his title, in the semi-final. He had won 43 singles in all, a dozen were in five sets, when he forsook Wimbledon for the professional ranks.

Cochet's Davis Cup career for France could hardly have been more distinguished. A fifth match victory against 'Little Bill' Johnston gave the trophy to France in 1927. He won two live singles in the Challenge Rounds in 1928, 1929, a live and a dead one in 1930, two live in 1931 and another live one in 1932. When he lost to Fred Perry in 1933 it was the key result that turned the trophy to Great Britain and away from France

As an unpredictable genius Cochet turned professional and though he was later reinstated as an amateur he was, under the rules then pertaining, barred from events like Wimbledon. He showed his sleepy and unique talents in the British Hard Court Championships in 1949 when at the age of 47 he reached the final against Pedro Masip of Spain.

It was of Cochet that the story was coined of his dreaming that he was playing on the Centre Court. When he woke up he found that he was!

Wimbledon Singles Record:

1922, won 3 matches, lost James Anderson, 4th round.

1923, 1924, did not play.

1925, won 5 matches, lost Jean Borotra, semi-final.

1926, won 5 matches, lost Jean Borotra, semi-final.

1927, seeded 4, won 7 matches, *champion* (sets 21–7; games 154–117).

1928, seeded 1, won 6 matches, lost Rene Lacoste, final.

1929, seeded 1, won 7 matches, *champion* (sets 21–3; games 147–95).

1930, seeded 1, won 4 matches, lost W. Allison, quarter-final.

1931, seeded 2, won 0 matches, lost Nigel Sharpe, 1st round.

1932, seeded 1, won 1 match, lost Ian Collins, 2nd round (won plate).

1933, seeded 3, won 5 matches, lost Ellsworth Vines, semi-final.

Matches: 43–8; sets 135–59; games 1058–786.

Longest Match: 1st round 1930, beat Henk Timmer 6–4 9–11 4–6 6–4 6–2 – a total of 58 games.

Age on first winning singles: 25 years 200 days.

Age on last winning singles: 27 years 204 days.

Overall Record:

	Titles	Matches Played	Won	Lost
Singles	2	51	43	8
Doubles	2	39	33	6
Mixed	0	29	21	8
Total	4	119	97	22

Career Achievements:

The Championships, Wimbledon: singles 1927, 1929; doubles 1926, 1928.

US Championships: singles 1928; mixed 1927.

French Championships: singles 1926, 1928, 1930, 1932; doubles 1927, 1930, 1932; mixed 1928, 1929.

Total Grand Slam titles: 15 – singles 7, doubles 5, mixed 3

Olympic Games: singles 1924 silver, doubles 1924 silver

French Davis Cup team: 1922–1924, 1926–1933, winning 44 from 58 matches (singles 34–8; doubles 10–6) in 26 ties.

Full name: Henri Jean Cochet

Born: 14th December, 1901, Villeurbanne, Lyons, France.

Died: 1st April, 1987, Paris, France.

Sidney Wood

1931

Youngster with a Walkover

Two distinctions belong to Sidney Wood. He was, at the age of 19 years 245 days, then the second youngest Gentlemen's singles victor after Wilfred Baddeley, who was 71 days younger as the champion of 1891. He was also the only champion to be given a walkover in the title match.

That happened because in 1931, when he was competing for the third time, Wood came through to a final against Frank Shields, his Davis Cup team colleague. Shields hurt his ankle. Since the USA was engaged to meet Great Britain in the Inter-Zone Final of the Davis Cup in Paris less than two weeks hence it was considered prudent to rest him.

Would Shields have won? The odds were that he would. He was the third seed, Wood the seventh, which was later to be their positions in the US ranking list for the season. Shields was one year older and though he had lost one more set (four) in reaching the final he had lost fewer games (66) than Wood (80). All in all Wood must rank as a lucky winner and the sacrifice of Shields proved in the end of no avail since Great Britain beat the USA in the tie in Paris.

The previous year Wood had been a semi-finalist in the US singles at Forest Hills. Shields was his conqueror by three sets to one. The best Wood did at Forest Hills was as losing finalist in 1935. His first appearance at Wimbledon was sensational. It was in 1927 when he was only 15 and clad in white knickerbockers. Meeting Rene Lacoste in the first round he won only four games. His highest ranking in the US list was number two in 1934. In his last appearance at Wimbledon in 1935 he lost a notable five setter against Australia's Jack Crawford.

Wimbledon Singles Record:
1927, unseeded, won 0 matches, lost Rene Lacoste, 1st round.
1928, unseeded, won 2 matches, lost Pierre Landry, 3rd round.
1929, 1930 did not play.
1931, seeded 7, won 6 matches, *champion* (sets 18–3; games 132–80).

1932, seeded 5, won 4 matches, lost Jiro Satoh, quarter-final.

1933, did not play.

1934, seeded 7, won 5 matches, lost Fred Perry, semi-final.

1935, seeded 6, won 4 matches, lost Jack Crawford, quarter-final.

Matches: 21–5; sets 69–25; games 536–384.

Longest Match: 4th round 1931, beat Camille Malfroy 6–3 10–12 10–8 6–4 – a total of 59 games.

Age on winning singles: 19 years 245 days.

Overall Record:

| | Titles | Matches | | |
		Played	Won	Lost
Singles	1	26	21	5
Doubles	0	19	13	6
Mixed	0	0	0	0
Total	1	45	34	11

Career Achievements:

The Championships, Wimbledon: singles 1931.

Total Grand Slam titles: 1 – singles 1.

US Davis Cup team: 1931, 1934, winning 8 from 14 matches (singles 5–6; doubles 3–0) in 7 ties.

Full name: Sidney Burr Beardslee Wood

Born: 1st November, 1911, Black Rock, Connecticut, USA.

Ellsworth Vines

1932

The Pacemaker

Of all the first time winners of the singles the most impressive was probably Ellsworth Vines, a meteoric victor in 1932. He was only 20 and he had won his own US singles the previous year. For the period in which he won in turn the US title, the Wimbledon crown and the US for the second time, it is arguable that no man hit the ball harder on his forehand and in serving.

His electrifying progress was symbolised by the shot with which he won his Wimbledon final against the British No. 2, Bunny Austin. He stood at match point at 40–15 with the match well won (the game score was 6–4 6–2 5–0) and rose on his toes as he tossed the ball to make for a more spectacular delivery than most. He swung at the ball and it seemed to vanish. There was a cloud of

dust from the service line, enough to convince the line judge that the ball was good. The back netting gyrated and down fell the ball. Austin, as he confessed after, knew not if the ball had passed his backhand or forehand. It was a cannon ball delivery to end all cannon ball deliveries and Vines was the champion.

It could be said that this angular Californian burnt himself out quickly. He defended his title in 1933, reached the final and was outplayed, after one of the finest contests of all time, by the Australian Jack Crawford. In October 1933 he turned professional. Later he became a professional golfer and was a top line player, though never to heights comparable to his prowess at lawn tennis.

In his peak spells his generation of pace both overhead on the service and from the forehand, was awesome and he became quite unplayable. His brief appearance at Wimbledon over two years was spectacular. So, too, was his last Davis Cup match for the US. In the Inter-Zone final tie against Great Britain in Paris in 1933, played at the Stade Roland Garros, where the slow surface and heat handicapped Vines more than most, he met Fred Perry in the fifth match and, when 6–7 and 15–40 on his service in the fifth set, collapsed and had to be carried away. Earlier he had lost to Austin.

At 21 he was past his best.

Wimbledon Singles Record:
1932, seeded 2, won 7 matches, *champion* (sets 21–2; games 135–68).
1933, seeded 1, won 6 matches, lost Jack Crawford, final.

Matches: 13–1; sets 41–8; games 283–162.

Longest Match: Final 1933, lost Jack Crawford 6–4 9–11 2–6 6–2 4–6 – a total of 56 games.

Age on winning singles: 20 years 278 days.

Overall Record:

	Titles	Matches Played	Won	Lost
Singles	1	14	13	1
Doubles	0	1	0	1
Mixed	0	3	3	0
Total	1	18	16	2

Career Achievements:
The Championships, Wimbledon: singles 1932
US Championships: singles 1931, 1932; doubles 1932; mixed 1933.
Australian Championships: doubles 1933.
Total Grand Slam titles: 6 – singles 3, doubles 2, mixed 1
US Davis Cup team: 1932–1933, winning 13 from 16 matches (singles 13–3) in 8 ties.

Full name: Henry Ellsworth Vines
Born: 28 September, 1911, Los Angeles, California, USA.
Died: 17 March, 1994, La Quinta, California, USA.

Jack Crawford

1933

Classical Fluency

Like another great player, Margaret Smith-Court, Jack Crawford was born in Albury, on the border between New South Wales and Victoria. His Wimbledon singles championship was nine years in the past when Margaret was born. It was nine years, too, since he had come within a two sets to one lead of being the first player to win the Grand Slam.

That was in 1933 when, already Australian, French and Wimbledon champion, he met Fred Perry in the final of the US Championships at Forest Hills. Perry beat him 6–3 11–13 4–6 6–0 6–1 and Crawford never was a winner of that title.

Crawford, even in the 1930s seemed out of his time. He favoured a racket which, with its flat top, looked old fashioned. He invariably wore a white shirt with the sleeves buttoned at the wrist and rolled up only to face some crisis. And, more than that, he had a flowing purity of stroke which had every 'old hand' of the 1930s recalling the classicism of the Doherty brothers. He was basically a baseliner but one with pace and bite.

In his third challenge at Wimbledon in 1932 he met Ellsworth Vines, then in his glorious peak year, and was badly beaten in the semi-finals, having put out Perry in the round before. A year later Crawford began with a long struggle against the Spaniard Enrique Maier. In five further rounds his classic strength was unchecked. Vines was the finalist. Up to that stage the Californian had never lost a singles at Wimbledon. The beauty, tension and excitement of that final became a Wimbledon legend. In what was a most glorious contest, with each man playing superbly, Crawford's superb control finally mastered the pace making of Vines. The score was 4–6 11–9 6–2 2–6 6–4 with every one of its 56 games a gem.

Crawford did not reach such a peak of achievement again. He was a losing finalist to Perry in 1934, a losing semi-finalist to the same man in 1935 and a losing quarter-finalist to Gottfried von Cramm in 1936. He returned to Wimbledon in 1947 for old time's sake.

Wimbledon Singles Record:
1930, unseeded, won 2 matches, lost Herman David, 3rd round.
1931, did not play.
1932, seeded 8, won 5 matches, lost Ellsworth Vines, semi-final.
1933, seeded 2, won 7 matches, *champion* (sets 21–6; games 154–107).
1934, seeded 1, won 6 matches, lost Fred Perry, final.
1935, seeded 3, won 5 matches, lost Fred Perry, semi-final.
1936, seeded 6, won 4 matches, lost Gottfried von Cramm, quarter-final.
1937, unseeded, won 4 matches, lost Gottfried von Cramm, quarter-final.
1938, 1939, 1946, did not play.
1947, unseeded, won 0 matches, lost Max Ellmer, 1st round.

Matches: 36–8; sets 115–48; games 911–705.

Longest Match: Final 1933 beat Ellsworth Vines 4–6 11–9 6–2 2–6 6–4 – a total of 56 games.

Age on winning singles: 25 years 107 days.

Overall Record:

	Titles	Matches Played	Won	Lost
Singles	1	44	36	8
Doubles	1	24	16	8
Mixed	1	17	14	3
Total	3	85	66	19

Career Achievements:
The Championships, Wimbledon: singles 1933; doubles 1935; mixed 1930.
French Championships: singles 1933; doubles 1935; mixed 1933.
Australian Championships: singles 1931–1933, 1935; doubles 1929, 1930, 1932, 1935; mixed 1931–1933.
Total Grand Slam titles: 17 – singles 6, doubles 6, mixed 5.
Italian Championships: doubles 1935.
Australian Davis Cup team: 1928, 1930, 1932–1937, winning 36 from 58 matches (singles 23–16, 1 unf; doubles 13–5) in 23 ties.

Full name: John Herbert (Jack) Crawford
Born: 22nd March, 1908, Albury, NSW, Australia.
Died: 10th September, 1991, Cassnock, NSW, Australia.

Fred Perry

1934, 1935, 1936

The British Thruster

Fred Perry came to Wimbledon in 1934 at the age of 25 with his first notable international success behind him. In the previous autumn he had won the US National singles, the first British victor there since Laurie Doherty in 1903, a gap of 30 years. It was 25 years since a British player had won the Wimbledon singles, Arthur Gore in 1909. Perry made no secret of his desire to be the best in the world. He was thrustingly ambitious, the product of the grammar school (in Ealing) rather than the public school which was the background for so many British players.

His game, too, was thrustful. His running forehand, whereby he took the ball going forward and very, very early, was risky in the extreme. It brought him much frustration in his early days and subsequently proved suicidal to the many British youngsters who tried to imitate him.

At Wimbledon ever increasing hopes had been dashed, especially in 1933 when he fell to the South African Norman Farquarson in the second round. It was his worst achievement in The Championships to date.

Yet a few weeks later his inspirational play brought Great Britain to its first triumph in the Davis Cup for 21 years. After beating Australia at Wimbledon the British team defeated the USA in the Inter-Zone Final in Paris. Perry, invincible in singles, went on to lead against France in the Challenge Round where his win against Henri Cochet (by 8–10 6–4 8–6 3–6 6–1) and Andre Merlin (in the decisive fifth match by 4–6 8–6 6–2 7–5) were crucial.

At Forest Hills in 1933 it was the win of Perry in the final over Jack Crawford (by 6–3 11–13 4–6 6–0 6–1) that denied the Australian his chance of being the first Grand Slam victor. Appropriately Perry later became the first man to win all four major titles, though not the Grand Slam since they were not won in the same year.

Perry was twice extended the full distance in taking his 1934 title at Wimbledon, by the Czech Roderick Menzel in the third round, and by the former champion, Sidney Wood, in the semi-finals. Menzel led two sets to one. Never was Perry pressed so much again at Wimbledon.

He beat Crawford, the holder, in the final. This was in three sets. The next year, when Perry was riding against all comers triumphantly, he beat Menzel in three sets in the quarter-finals and Crawford in four in the semis. He mastered the German Baron Gottfried von Cramm in the final in three sets.

In 1936 Perry beat Don Budge, just verging on his greatness, in the semi-finals. In the title match, the last singles Perry played in The Championships, he again beat von Cramm. But it was a hollow victory since the German hurt his ankle in the opening game.

A little later the Centre Court saw Perry in Davis Cup action in the Challenge Round against Australia. His invincibility was never threatened. He thus ended four years of unchecked Davis Cup success and three years in The Championships where he had won three successive titles and taken 21 consecutive singles. The record stood for a long time. After taking his third US singles title in four years Perry turned professional. There never was a more effectively thrustful British player. He became an American citizen and served in the US forces in World War II. He died in Australia in February 1995.

Wimbledon Singles Record:
1929, unseeded, won 2 matches, lost lost John Olliff, 3rd round.
1930, unseeded, won 3 matches, lost Colin Gregory, 4th round.
1931, seeded 5, won 5 matches, lost Sidney Wood, semi-final.
1932, seeded 4, won 4 matches, lost Jack Crawford, quarter-final.
1933, seeded 6, won 1 match, lost Norman Farquharson, second round.
1934, seeded 2, won 7 matches, *champion* (sets 21–6; games 153–101).
1935, seeded 1, won 7 matches, *champion* (sets 21–3; games 141–79).
1936, seeded 1, won 7 matches, *champion* (sets 21–1; games 131–56).

Matches: 36–5; sets 115–31; games 826–536.

Longest Match: 1st round 1929, beat Roberto Bocciardo 7–5 2–6 6–4 3–6 9–7 – a total of 55 games.

Age on first winning singles: 25 years 49 days.

Age on last winning singles: 27 years 46 days.

Overall Record:

	Titles	Matches		
		Played	*Won*	*Lost*
Singles	3	41	36	5
Doubles	0	17	12	5
Mixed	2	15	13	2
Total	5	73	61	12

Career Achievements:
The Championships, Wimbledon: singles 1934–1936; mixed 1935, 1936.
US Championships: singles 1933, 1934, 1936; mixed 1932.
French Championships: singles 1935; doubles 1933; mixed 1932.
Australian Championships: singles 1934; doubles 1934.
Total Grand Slam titles: 14 – singles 8, doubles 2, mixed 4.
British Davis Cup team: 1931–1936, winning 45 from 52 matches (singles 34–4; doubles 11–3) in 20 ties.

Full name: Frederick John Perry
Born: 18th May, 1909, Stockport, Cheshire, England.
Died: 2nd February, 1995, Melbourne, Victoria, Australia.

Donald Budge

1937, 1938

Supreme Champion

Don Budge, a red headed Californian and son of a Glasgow Rangers soccer player who had been badly injured at the game, has an assured place in the story of the first one hundred years of lawn tennis on more than one count.

He was the first player to hold all four major singles championships, those of Australia, France, Wimbledon and the USA at the same time. He achieved that in the spring of 1938 when he became champion of France. He went on to complete a Grand Slam by retaining his Wimbledon and US titles that year. The only other man to win all four major titles in the same year is Rod Laver, and the Australian achieved that remarkable feat twice – as a amateur in 1962 and in 1969 as a professional. At the end of 1938 Budge turned professional to open a new chapter in his life.

This formidable American was the heroic winner of what was claimed at the time as the best match ever staged. It was in the Davis Cup tie between the USA and Germany in the Inter-Zone final on the Centre Court at Wimbledon in 1937. In the fifth and decisive match against Gottfried von Cramm Budge trailed 2–5 in the fifth set It was a contest of sustained brilliance, each projecting positive shots and each spurred by the opposition quality to more and more virtuosity. Budge eventually won 6–8 5–7 6–4 6–2 8–6. The subsequent Challenge Round against Great Britain was a formality.

In the context of Wimbledon, Budge was twice the triple champion, in 1937 and 1938. In 1938 he lost no set in the singles and dropped a total of only 48 games in his seven rounds. Indeed the only set he lost that year was one in the Gentlemen's doubles with Gene Mako. His mixed partner was Alice Marble. His total Wimbledon tally in 1938 was: matches 19–0: sets 51–1; games 325–142.

He won Wimbledon at his third attempt, losing in the semi-finals of the singles in 1935 and 1936 to Gottfried von Cramm and Fred Perry respectively. In 1937 he lost one set, to the American Frank Parker, in the semi-finals. In the final he mastered von Cramm, who was playing that match for the third year, readily. His 1938 triumph was complete. Only thrice did he play an advantage set in singles and the British finalist, Bunny Austin, won fewer games against him than when overwhelmed by Ellsworth Vines seven years earlier.

In the course of his Grand Slam sequence, that is to say Wimbledon and the US Championships 1937, the Australian, French, Wimbledon and US Championships 1938, Budge won 37 matches, 111 sets. He lost only 8 sets in all and only twice was he taken the full distance. His heavyweight progress was awesome in its consistency and authority.

He was aggressive to a degree, with weight of shot all round. Possibly there was some chink to be found on the forehand side but that was because he was less strong there than on the other wing. His backhand drive was a dream, a heavy, killing shot in which he had supreme confidence. He used a heavy racket – 15 ounces – and, tending to support it with his other hand until the last moment. he developed a rolled shot which was accurate and devastating.

Some have held Budge to have been the greatest player of all time during the era of wooden raquets. He and Big Bill Tilden would certainly be among the first to be considered in such an assessment.

Wimbledon Singles Record:
1935, unseeded, won 5 matches, lost lost Gottfried von Cramm, semi-final.
1936, seeded 5, won 5 matches, lost Fred Perry, semi-final.
1937, seeded 1, won 7 matches, *champion* (sets 21–1; games 128–59).
1938, seeded 1, won 7 matches, *champion* (sets 21–0; games 129–48).

Matches: 24–2; sets 74–91; games 485–247.

Longest Match: Quarter-final 1935, beat Henry Austin 3–6 10–8 6–4 7–5 – a total of 49 games.

Age on first winning singles: 22 years 19 days.

Age on last winning singles: 23 years 18 days.

Overall Record:

	Titles	Matches Played	Won	Lost
Singles	2	26	24	2
Doubles	2	19	18	1
Mixed	2	18	17	1
Total	6	63	59	4

Career Achievements:
The Championships, Wimbledon: singles 1937, 1938; doubles 1937, 1938; mixed 1937, 1938.
US Championships: singles 1937, 1938; doubles 1936, 1938; mixed 1937, 1938.
French Championships: singles 1938.
Australian Championships: singles 1938.
Total Grand Slam titles: 14 – singles 6, doubles 4, mixed 4.
    The first winner of the 'Grand Slam'.
US Davis Cup team: 1935–1938, winning 25 from 29 matches (singles 19–2; doubles 6–2) in 11 ties.

Full name: John Donald Budge
Born: 13th June, 1915, Oakland, California, USA.
Died: 20th January, 2000, Scranton, Pennsylvania, USA.

Bobby Riggs

1939

The Hustler

Bobby Riggs, the fourth Californian and the sixth American to win the singles, holds a unique place in the history of The Championships. He competed but once and is the only player to have competed in all three events and never been beaten.

He was a versatile, touch player and an astute tactician. Prior to the final of the singles at Wimbledon the only man to press him was the British player Ron Shayes, who was killed in the war. In the last match Riggs met his compatriot Ellwood Cooke, who built a lead of two sets to one to no avail. Indeed, in hindsight it was remarked that Riggs had trailed in such matches before. He was said to have backed himself to win all three events at Wimbledon. Cooke was his men's doubles partner and in that event the crux was a dangerous two sets to one lead built in the quarter-finals against them by the British pair Henry Billington and Pat Hughes.

His mixed partner was Alice Marble, herself a triple champion that year. There was one hundred per cent American success at the 1939 Wimbledon with only four players involved, Riggs, Miss Marble, Cooke and Sarah Fabyan.

Riggs won the US title later in 1939. He took it for the second time in 1941 but because of the war he had no long career in the international game. He became a professional.

After the war he could not match the talents of younger rivals who used the Wimbledon and US titles as the launching point to their money careers. In his fifties he took on the role as the apostle of 'male chauvinism' by playing Margaret Court in San Diego in 1973 in May. It was no surprise when he proved the superiority of male muscle power in winning 6–2 6–1. But he sadly marred his case when in September he met the challenge of Billie Jean King and lost 4–6 3–6 3–6 at Houston before a crowd of 30,492 and with a purse of $100,000.

Wimbledon Singles Record:

1939, seeded 2, won 7 matches, *champion* (sets 21–3; games 147–92).

Matches: 7–0; sets 21–3; games 147–92.

Longest Match: Final 1939, beat Elwood Cooke 2–6 8–6 3–6 6–3 6–2 – a total of 48 games.

Age on winning singles: 21 years 132 days.

Overall Record:

	Titles	Matches Played	Won	Lost
Singles	1	7	7	0
Doubles	1	6	6	0
Mixed	1	6	6	0
Total	3	19	19	0

Career Achievements:

The Championships, Wimbledon: singles 1939; doubles 1939; mixed 1939.
US Championships: singles 1939, 1941; mixed 1940.
Total Grand Slam titles: 6 – singles 3, doubles 1, mixed 2
US Davis Cup team: 1938–1939, winning 2 from 4 matches (singles 2–2) in 2 ties.

Full name: Robert Larimore Riggs
Born: 25th February, 1918, Los Angeles, California, USA.
Died: 25th October, 1995, Leucadia, California, USA.

Yvon Petra

1946

The Gallic Giant

When The Championships resumed in 1946, Yvon Petra unexpectedly and temporarily revived the tradition of French supremacy, made up by the resounding successes of Jean Borotra, Rene Lacoste and Henri Cochet in the between war years. He can hardly be said to have come out of the blue when his burly frame and heavy shots had their success, for he was the number five seed at a Wimbledon which combined post-war austerity with the euphoria of starting up again; it seemed probable that if Dinny Pails of Australia did not win then Jack Kramer, a striking American, would.

Kramer fell victim to a blistered hand and the wiles of the Czech Jaroslav Drobny. Pails had the misfortune to lose his way on London's Underground and arrived to play his quarter-final in the panic of late arrival. The man who took advantage of his upset was Petra.

It opened the way to one of the most surprising wins on record. Petra took his chances ably. Having beaten Pails in four sets (7–5 7–5 6–8 6–4) he beat the American Tom Brown in five (4–6 4–6 6–3 7–5 8–6). He lived dangerously. In the final he met the other Brown, Geoff Brown of Australia. Brown was small, double fisted on the forehand and with one of the fastest services ever delivered. It was a muddled final, for Geoff Brown originally followed the mistaken advice to slow Petra up – with Petra, a Frenchman, a clay court man! Petra emerged the victor by 6–2 6–4 7–9 5–7 6–4.

It was not Petra's first Wimbledon visit. He was there in 1936 and 1937, though without particular distinction. Before the war he had won the doubles in his own Championships and established himself as a Davis Cup man.

Petra defended his title in 1947 but met Tom Brown in the quarter-finals and got no further. He became a professional in 1948 and for many years was settled in the USA.

Wimbledon Singles Record:

1936, unseeded, won 2 matches, lost Donald Butler, 3rd round.

1937, unseeded, won 0 matches, lost Frank Wilde, 1st round.

1938, 1939, did not play.

1946, seeded 5, won 7 matches, *champion* (sets 21–6; games 167–115).

1947, seeded 7, won 4 matches, lost Thomas Brown, quarter-final

Matches: 13–3; sets 42–16; games 334–238.

Longest Match: Final 1946, beat Geoffrey Brown 6–2 6–4 7–9 5–7 6–4 – a total of 56 games.

Age on winning singles: 30 years 119 days.

Overall Record:

	Titles	Matches		
		Played	Won	Lost
Singles	1	16	13	3
Doubles	0	12	8	4
Mixed	0	11	8	3
Total	1	39	29	10

Career Achievements:

The Championships, Wimbledon: singles 1946.

French Championships: doubles 1938, 1946; mixed 1937.

Total Grand Slam titles: 4 – singles 1, doubles 2, mixed 1.

French Davis Cup team: 1937–1939, winning 15 from 22 matches (singles 11–3; doubles 4–4) in 12 ties.

Full name: Yvon Francois Marie Petra

Born: 8th March, 1916, Cholon, Indo-China.

Died: 12th September, 1984, Paris, France.

Jack Kramer

1947

Emphatic and Brief

Ever since Jack Kramer appeared at Wimbledon, in 1946 and 1947, many have felt that this superb American could, had he wished, have built a record that would have secured an obvious place among the very greatest in the game. But he was anxious to capitalize his skill in the professional ranks and he did so as soon as he had proved himself the best of the amateurs.

He would have turned professional had he won Wimbledon in 1946. Once he had shown his mastery in the early rounds it became obvious then that the chances were that he would. In reaching the third round he had lost a total of only six games in the three matches. He then met the Czech Jaroslav Drobny, whose left-handed service was then at its most deadly, and had the bad luck to have to play with a badly blistered hand. His big grip and 16 ounce racket did not help! Consequently Kramer was beaten over five sets and a total of 67 games. Going back to the US he won the National Singles at Forest Hills for the loss of one set.

His return to Wimbledon in 1947 was as outstanding favourite. His progress was sweeping. With five wins behind him he arrived in the semi-finals for the total loss of only 23 games. At that stage he met the Australian Dinny Pails in what the seeding had forecast as the final for the preceding year. Pails won the second set – and Kramer won the other three for the loss of two games!

In the final against his compatriot, Tom Brown, Kramer won 6–1 6–3 6–2 in 48 minutes, the most one sided and quickest win there, injuries apart, of modern times. Kramer was overwhelmingly dominant in every department of his heavyweight aggressive game. He seemed as near perfect as a man could be.

The upshot was the most complete Wimbledon singles victory ever achieved by a man playing through, despite the loss of one set. Kramer's tally, 130 games to 37, has never been surpassed in the sparsity of lost games. He won 77% of all the games he played!

A few weeks later Kramer won his own title for the second time and became professional. He had notable success as a professional player. He had even more success as a promoter and, when the Open game came about in 1968, was a leading architect of the Grand Prix.

Kramer had indicated his potential before the war. As an 18-year-old he was one of the US side, albeit only in the doubles, who let slip the Challenge Round tie against Australia after a lead of 2–love. When he played in the two post war years he never lost a singles and with his six out of six record the US firmly regained the trophy.

He was the powerful advocate of 'percentage play'. That is to say that in any situation the shot to be played was that most likely to be successful, the risks minimal. No man played it better.

Wimbledon Singles Record:
1946, seeded 2, won 3 matches, lost Jaroslav Drobny, 4th round.
1947, seeded 1, won 7 matches, *champion* (sets 21–1; games 130–37).

Matches: 10–1; sets 32–4; games 217–76.

Longest Match: 4th round 1946, lost Jaroslav Drobny 6–2 15–17 3–6 6–3 3–6 – a total of 67 games.

Age on winning singles: 25 years 337 days.

Overall Record:

	Titles	Matches Played	Won	Lost
Singles	1	11	10	1
Doubles	2	12	12	0
Mixed	0	0	0	0
Total	3	23	22	1

Career Achievements:
The Championships, Wimbledon: singles 1947; doubles 1946, 1947.
US Championships: singles 1946, 1947; doubles 1940, 1941, 1943, 1947; mixed 1941.
Total Grand Slam titles: 10 – singles 3, doubles 6, mixed 1
US Davis Cup team: 1939, 1946–1947, winning 7 from 9 matches (singles 6–0; doubles 1–2) in 4 ties.

Full name: John Albert Kramer
Born: 1st August 1921, Las Vegas, Nevada, USA.

Bob Falkenburg

1948

Praying Mantis

Like Yvon Petra, two years before, but unlike Jack Kramer who won in 1947 as one of the strongest favourites of all time, the lanky Bob Falkenburg was an unexpected winner in 1948. He came from California, albeit born in New York, and he gave the impression that every match would be his last.

This was because of his way of playing. For him conservation of energy was vital, so much so that it was not unknown for him to cast away whole sets while he recouped. His occasional habit of falling to his knees on court led to his being called 'The Praying Mantis'.

He had a powerful service. It was his main lifeline. But he was also a splendid match player, never better – and never more ready to try a hit or miss stroke – in a crisis.

In his second appearance at Wimbledon after being a quarter-finalist the year before, Falkenburg looked like losing to the Yugoslav Dragutin Mitic in the third round. He survived after trailing one set to two in the 50th game. His adventures there were nothing to the final.

The Australian John Bromwich, double fisted on the forehand and a supreme touch player, opposed him. Bromwich was seeded two and, had he won, no more popular victory would have been had. He was a player spectators loved. Falkenburg they did not, mainly because of his habit of 'stalling', which was held to be unsporting. The final, a splendid tussle, veered this way and that. Eventually the magic touch of Bromwich took him to 5–2 in the fifth set. At 5–3 he led 40–15. Bromwich had three match points in all. On two of them Falkenburg projected his service return with an express shot across the court that was an utter gamble. The other was a backhand pass down the line that Falkenburg hit as he slid, out of balance, and down on one knee. Bromwich, well placed at the net, lifted his racket as if to play

the volley but left it, only to see it land on the sideline. It was a heartbreaking moment. Bromwich had no more chances and Falkenburg was the champion.

When he defended next year he lost to Bromwich in the quarter-finals. Falkenburg's Wimbledon career was explosive and exciting.

It was in 1949, when he still had the status of Wimbledon singles champion, that Falkenburg played a match that one would hardly expect from one with lack of stamina. In Los Angeles he partnered Ted Schroeder (who was a few weeks later his successor as Wimbledon champion) in a memorable doubles in which they beat Pancho Gonzales and Hugh Stewart 36–34 3–6 4–6 6–4 19–17. It lasted four hours 45 minutes. It stood as the world record for the greatest number of games in a match until another US pair played even more in 1967.

Falkenburg was also a Davis Cup man, though not for the US He qualified by residence for Brazil and led their side in 1954 and 1955; in the first year it was against Great Britain at Eastbourne. He took the opportunity of playing again at Wimbledon but lost in the 3rd round to Ken Rosewall.

By his style of play and by his knife edge victory he was a memorable champion.

Wimbledon Singles Record:
1947, seeded 8, won 4 matches, lost Dinny Pails, quarter-final.
1948, seeded 7, won 7 matches, *champion* (sets 21–5; games 145–97)
1949, seeded 4, won 4 matches, lost John Bromwich, quarter-final.
1950–1953, did not play.
1954, unseeded won 2 matches, lost Kenneth Rosewall, 3rd round.

Matches: 17–3; sets 56–17; games 388–289.

Longest Match: Quarter-final 1949, lost to John Bromwich 6–3 11–9 0–6 0–6 4–6 – a total of 51 games.

Age on winning singles: 22 years 155 days.

Overall Record:

	Titles	Matches Played	Won	Lost
Singles	1	20	17	3
Doubles	1	19	15	4
Mixed	0	3	2	1
Total	2	42	34	8

Career Achievements:
The Championships, Wimbledon: singles 1948; doubles 1947.
US Championships: doubles 1944.
Total Grand Slam titles: 3 – singles 1, doubles 2
Brazilian Davis Cup team: 1954, 1955, winning 3 from 10 matches (singles 2–4; doubles 1–3) in 4 ties.

Full name: Robert (Bob) Falkenburg
Born: 29th January, 1926, New York, New York, USA.

Ted Schroeder

1949

The Bold Adventurer

With a pipe always on the go, with a rolling gait that would have made him look at home on the deck of a schooner, with a sun tanned face and a happy grin 'Lucky' Ted Schroeder came from California in 1949 with cheerful and wholly successful abandon. He was one of those rare visitors who came just once and never knew what it was like to lose a singles.

Not that he did not come perilously close to it. His initial match in the singles was in itself a sensation. He was seeded one and his doubles partner, Gardnar Mulloy, whose personality and skill was almost as strong as his own, might have been a seed as well. But Mulloy was overlooked and they clashed in the first round. Schroeder lost the first two sets and the second went to 20 games. Then he showed that all the stamina was his and he lost only four games in the remainder of the match. His greater peril was to come.

That was on the first Saturday when he met the Australian Frank Sedgman in the quarter-finals on No. 1 Court. Sedgman had touch and power in rich combination. He won the first two sets. He led 5–4 in the fifth and Schroeder, serving, was 30–40, match point down. He was foot faulted. Then he came up to the net on his second serve and volleyed a brilliant winner. He saved a second match point at 5–6 with a fine backhand. Schroeder, the coolest man on court, survived after a memorable battle of 56 games.

In the semi-finals Schroeder recouped a one set to two deficit against the South African Eric Sturgess. In the final he beat Jaroslav Drobny in five sets after losing the first. In all he became champion after losing eight sets and no champion had yielded so many until Boris Becker in 1985.

His men's doubles almost paralleled his singles adventures. With Mulloy he saved two match balls in the fifth set against Geoff Brown and Bill Sidwell in the semi-finals. But they lost, tamely by comparison, to Ricardo Gonzales and Frank Parker in the final.

At a time when most top players, even if technically amateur, were becoming more and more professional in their attitude and schedules, the popular Ted Schroeder maintained an independence that was as rugged as his play. In the immediate post-war US Championships 1946 to 1948 he declined to compete while at the same time his invincibility was a major reason for American triumph in the Challenge Round of the Davis Cup.

Having won Wimbledon he did compete at Forest Hills in 1949 – he had been a war time victor in 1942 – and yielded to Gonzales in the final. But Wimbledon never saw him again, not as a player.

Prior to the 1949 Championships he had sampled the quality of British turf in the London title meeting at Queen's Club. He won. He never lost a singles in his three week visit.

Wimbledon Singles Record:
1949, seeded 1, won 7 matches, *champion* (21–8; games 172–119).

Matches: 7–0; sets 21–8; games 172–119.

Longest Match: Quarter-final 1949, beat Frank Sedgman 3–6 6–8 6–3 6–2 9–7 – a total of 56 games.

Age on winning singles: 27 years 346 days.

Overall Record:

	Titles	Matches Played	Won	Lost
Singles	1	7	7	0
Doubles	0	6	5	1
Mixed	0	1	0	1
Total	1	14	12	2

Career Achievements:
The Championships, Wimbledon: singles 1949.
US Championships: singles 1942; doubles 1940, 1941, 1947; mixed 1942.
Total Grand Slam titles: 6 – singles 2, doubles 3, mixed 1.
US Davis Cup team: 1946–1951, winning 13 from 19 matches (singles 11–3; doubles 2–3) in 8 ties.

Full name: Frederick Rudolph (Ted) Schroeder
Born: 20th July, 1921, Newark, New Jersey, USA.

Budge Patty

1950

Player in Training

Budge Patty, then a Private, First Class in the American Army, made himself as a player with high potential when in 1945, after the end of hostilities in Europe, he won an Allied Forces tournament in Marseilles. Subsequently his status was as a GI who had stayed behind in Europe. As a friend, and a handsome one, of polish and good manners, of many notables he was well known in what could be termed 'café society' of the continent.

With his ease and economy of style and beautiful touch he perfected a game of exquisite brilliance. In the context of Wimbledon his popularity amounted towards idolatry. He made a mark at his first challenge in 1946 when he got to the last 16. The next year he was a force to be reckoned with. He beat the second seeded John Bromwich, then the sixth seeded Jaroslav Drobny before falling in the semi-finals to Tom Brown.

In this and subsequent years the question posed about Patty was his fitness. He was said to find late nights better than training. But in 1950 all went well. He cut out his smoking. His reward was to win the French Championships (he beat Drobny in the final), having lost in the last match the year before. At Wimbledon he had a four setter in the opening round, and three more very hard four set matches in the last three stages, beating in sequence his fellow Americans William Talbert and Vic Seixas before out playing the Australian Frank Sedgeman in the final. He might have been British for the warmth which greeted his wins.

His air was never American and he rarely played in the US. It was subsequent to his singles win that he imprinted himself deeper into Wimbledon memories. In 1953 he met Drobny in the third round. Their singles rivalry was acute. They were well matched and had met often, indeed they were travelling companions around the continental circuits.

Their historic contest began around 5 o'clock, the second match on the Centre Court. By about nine twenty, when light was almost gone, one of the finest and most keenly fought battles came to an end. Drobny was the victor – just.

He won 8–6 16–18 3–6 8–6 12–10 and few of those 93 games, the greatest number at that time played at Wimbledon, were anything but a high quality serve and volley attack. Patty had six match points in the course of it.

In that Patty was a hero in defeat. In 1957 he was a hero again, this time as an unexpected victor. This was in doubles not singles. His partner was Gardnar Mulloy. Patty was 33, Mulloy was 43. With so high a combined age their chances in the event seemed slim. Nonetheless their craft took them through and in the final they met two Australians, Neale Fraser and Lew Hoad, who were in their prime. Despite the disparity in age Patty and Mulloy had the victory, made all the more exciting because Queen Elizabeth II was watching. Her presence provoked an eccentric middle aged woman to run across the Centre Court with a banner of protest about the iniquities of international banking. Mulloy became the oldest man to win a Wimbledon title.

Patty went on at Wimbledon and did not play his last singles until 1960. He ended with a fine record of success and with the reputation as the possessor of the best forehand volleys of all time.

Later he married and settled down as a Swiss business man, more European than American by far. He was hardly known in the US as a player, except when a junior. In 1951 he played in the US Championships, where he was a quarter-finalist, and played for the US in the same year with fleeting Davis Cup duty in one tie against Canada. He was also a quarter-finalist at Forest Hills in 1953. They knew him better at the Stade Roland Garros in Paris.

Wimbledon Singles Record:
1946, unseeded, won 3 matches, lost Dinny Pails, 4th round.
1947, unseeded, won 5 matches, lost Thomas Brown, semi-final.
1948, seeded 6, won 4 matches, lost John Bromwich, quarter-final.
1949, unseeded, won 2 matches, lost Jaroslav Drobny, 3rd round.
1950, seeded 5, won 7 matches, *champion* (21–4; games 154–97).
1951, seeded 4, won 1 match, lost Hamilton Richardson, 2nd round.
1952, seeded 12, won 3 matches, lost Victor Seixas, 4th round.
1953, unseeded, won 2 matches, lost Jaroslav Drobny, 3rd round.
1954, seeded 7, won 5 matches, lost Jaroslav Drobny, semi-final.
1955, seeded 7, won 5 matches, lost Tony Trabert, semi-final.
1956, seeded 4, won 1 match, lost Bobby Wilson, 2nd round.
1957, unseeded, won 3 matches, lost Neale Fraser, 4th round.
1958, unseeded, won 3 matches, lost Sven Davidson, 4th round.
1959, unseeded, won 0 matches, lost Jon Douglas, 1st round.
1960, unseeded, won 0 matches, lost Nicola Pietrangeli, 1st round.

Matches: 44–14; sets 143–65; games 1,163–901.

Longest Match: 3rd round 1953, lost Jaroslav Drobny 6–8 18–16 6–3 6–8 10–12 – a total of 93 games.

Age on winning singles: 26 years 146 days.

Overall Record:

	Titles	Matches Played	Won	Lost
Singles	1	58	44	14
Doubles	1	51	39	12
Mixed	0	10	8	2
Total	1	119	91	28

Career Achievements:
The Championships, Wimbledon: singles 1950; doubles 1957.
French Championships: singles 1950; mixed 1946
Total Grand Slam titles: 4 – singles 2, doubles 1, mixed 1
Italian Championships: singles 1954.
US Davis Cup team: 1951, winning 2 from 2 matches (singles 1–0; doubles 1–0) in 1 tie.

Full name: John Edward (Budge) Patty
Born: 11th February, 1924, Fort Smith, Arkansas, USA.

Richard Savitt

1951

American Nonconformist

Dick Savitt, from neither California nor Florida but New Jersey just across the river from New York City, was one of the rare bodies who won the men's singles at his first attempt. He defended his title a year later, 1952, as far as the quarter-finals. He was biggish in build, albeit with a hint of a stoop, and had a heavyweight backhand which was deliberate in action and quite punishing.

Had the game been open and given him the chance of being a full time player, one suspects that Savitt would have made a more permanent mark on the game. As it was he had a meteoric year in 1951. He began by winning the Australian title, was a forceful quarter-finalist against Jaroslav Drobny in Paris and then came out the winner at Wimbledon.

He had a crisis match against the Dane Kurt Nielsen in the third round, winning 6–4 in the fifth set against that giant killer who became an unseeded finalist in 1953 and 1955. The key to the championship was turned in the semi-final when he beat his compatriot Herbert Flam, like himself more of a baseliner than a volleyer. There was a surging, exciting second set and when Savitt eventually prised the 28th game from Flam's grasp, he was on a victory course. In the final he beat the Australian Ken McGregor, the man he had beaten to take the Australian title.

Later that year Savitt made a brief appearance for the US in the Davis Cup against Japan and Canada. Yet for the vital Challenge Round against Australia, in Australia where he had won the title twelve months before, the US selectors ignored him.

He made another world tour in 1952 but with less success. McGregor took away his Australian title. He lost again in Paris in the quarter-finals, to the South

African, Eric Sturgess. His status as title holder earned him no higher seeding place than four at Wimbledon. In the event he did not justify that, for he lost to the touch skills of Mervyn Rose in the quarters.

In his own national meeting at Forest Hills, easy commuting distance for Savitt from his home in South Orange, New Jersey, he did not get beyond the semi-finals. He reached that stage for the second year when he was the top seed in 1951. He had a quarter-final against Ken Rosewall in 1956 when his splendid backhand was matched by one that was supreme. The Australian won by 6–4 7–5 4–6 8–10 6–1.

But somehow Savitt was never a front runner within the US game. He was probably a better Wimbledon champion than is generally acknowledged.

Wimbledon Singles Record:
1951, seeded 6, won 7 matches, *champion* (21–3; games 145–90).
1952, seeded 4, won 4 matches, lost Mervyn Rose, quarter-final.

Matches: 11–1; sets 35–7; games 244–151.

Longest Match: Semi-final 1951, beat Herbie Flam 1–6 15–13 6–3 6–2 – a total of 52 games.

Age on winning singles: 24 years 124 days.

Overall Record:

	Titles	Matches Played	Won	Lost
Singles	1	12	11	1
Doubles	0	8	6	2
Mixed	0	0	0	0
Total	1	20	17	3

Career Achievements:
The Championships, Wimbledon: singles 1951.
Australian Championships: singles 1951.
Total Grand Slam titles: 2 – singles 2.
US Davis Cup team: 1951, winning 3 from 3 matches (singles 3–0) in 3 ties.

Full name: Richard Savitt
Born: 4th March, 1927, Bayonne, New Jersey, USA.

Frank Sedgman

1952

Feline Grace

After five successive years in which Americans seemed to be establishing a perpetual US copyright in the men's singles in line with their womenfolk, Frank Sedgman re-asserted the quality of the Australian game and became the fourth generation of his nation to win. He was a most satisfying player, for he moved about the court with the ease and grace of a cat and volleyed effortlessly.

His quality was outstanding and it combined with a gentle, sporting demeanour to make him one of the most popular champions. He won at his 5th attempt, having twice disappointed as the number one seed.

Sedgman arrived in the final in 1950. On form he should have won but he had had two difficult rounds. In the quarter-finals he recovered from a two sets to nil deficit against the American touch artist, Arthur Larsen. Only one set did not go to advantage games and its 63 games were the longest Sedgman had to endure at Wimbledon. Then in the semi-finals he again dropped the two opening sets before hauling himself through against Jaroslav Drobny. In the final Budge Patty surprisingly beat him. In that clash between two highly popular personalities the crowd had conflicting loyalties.

Again the top seed in 1951, Sedgman led the American Herbert Flam two sets to nil and lost an uneven quarter-final, disturbed by the weather. But a year later Sedgman came into his glorious own and from first to last cleared the Wimbledon hurdles as an unthreatened front runner. Drobny, who had half killed him two years before, was his final victim.

Thus Sedgman crowned his career. He was already holder of the US title and he went across the Atlantic to take that again. He was expected then to turn professional for if ever a man seemed entitled to turn his talents into a rewarding contract it was he. Curiously he delayed the inevitable and in so doing illustrated the complexities of finding resources while technically remaining amateur. It happened that he was getting married. He had already twice been the main instrument in Australia's Davis Cup successes. He was able to do so for the third time when the Australian ruling body gave him a wedding present of substantial proportions. No-one begrudged him his luck.

Wimbledon Singles Record:
1948, unseeded, won 3 matches, lost Robert Falkenburg, 4th round.
1949, seeded 8, won 4 matches, lost Ted Schroeder, quarter-final.
1950, seeded 1, won 6 matches, lost Budge Patty, final.
1951, seeded 1, won 4 matches, lost Herbie Flam, quarter-final.
1952, seeded 1, won 7 matches, *champion* (21–2; games 136–57).
1953–1970, did not play.
1971, unseeded, won 2 matches, lost Jeff Borowiak, 3rd round.
1972, did not play.
1973, unseeded, won 0 matches, lost Jiri Hrebec, 1st round.

Matches: 26–6; sets 84–31; games 640–462.

Longest Match: Quarter-final 1950, beat Art Larsen 8–10 5–7 7–5 6–3 7–5 – a total of 63 games.

Age on winning singles: 24 years 249 days.

Overall Record:

	Titles	Matches		
		Played	Won	Lost
Singles	1	32	26	6
Doubles	3	28	24	4
Mixed	2	30	26	4
Total	6	90	76	14

Career Achievements:
The Championships, Wimbledon: singles 1952; doubles 1948, 1951, 1952; mixed 1951, 1952.
US Championships: singles 1951, 1952; doubles 1950, 1951; mixed 1951, 1952.
French Championships: doubles 1951, 1952; mixed 1951, 1952.
Australian Championships: singles 1949, 1950; doubles 1951, 1952; mixed 1949, 1950.
Total Grand Slam titles: 22 – singles 5, doubles 9, mixed 8.
Italian Championships: singles 1952; doubles 1952.
Australian Davis Cup team: 1949–1952, winning 25 from 28 matches (singles 16–3; doubles 9–0) in 10 ties.

Full name: Francis Arthur (Frank) Sedgman
Born: 29th October, 1927, Mount Albert, Victoria, Australia.

Vic Seixas

1953

Relentless and Rugged

Like a famous predecessor, William Tilden, Victor Seixas was a son of Philadelphia. Like Tilden he was a 'late developer' and did not achieve his ultimate success as the Wimbledon singles champion until he was nearly 30 years old. That was in 1953 and it was not until a year later that he won his own national singles for the first time.

He was not a subtle, touch player, rather a rugged campaigner, prepared to go on and on until the opposition defences were eroded by the consistency of his pressure at the net. He was a superb competitor, respected and feared by all his rivals.

He made the grade as the top ranked US player in 1951. He had the same ranking (it was for the third time) in 1957, that for the season in which he turned 33.

During his Wimbledon visit in 1950 he was a surprise winner over John Bromwich in the fourth round and then beat the South African Eric Sturgess after a long quarter-final of 59 games. He then lost to Budge Patty in the semi-finals in four sets.

He was the top seed when he paid his third visit in 1953. He had a tremendous quarter-final against Lew Hoad, winning 5–7 6–4 6–3 1–6 9–7, then an even more rugged semi-final against another Australian, Mervyn Rose. Seixas won 6–4 10–12 9–11 6–4 6–3. He had a simple final against the Dane, Kurt Neilsen, as rugged but less skilled than himself, who was in the title match unseeded.

His next best performance was in 1956. He lost a memorable semi-final against Ken Rosewall, the Australian master winning 6–3 3–6 6–8 6–3 7–5. It was a match of historic quality.

One aspect of his achievement was noteworthy. Seixas took the mixed title in four consecutive years, 1953 to 1955 with Doris Hart and 1956 with Shirley Fry. He and Miss Hart were virtually invincible.

In the Davis Cup he played 55 matches for the USA, more than anyone until the arrival of John McEnroe in the late 1970s. He was in the Champion side of 1954 when he and Tony Trabert were irresistible.

He won his own national singles at his 9th attempt, a doughty effort.

Wimbledon Singles Record:
1950, seeded 12, won 5 matches, lost Budge Patty, semi-final.
1951, did not play.
1952, seeded 3, won 4 matches, lost Herbie Flam, quarter-final.
1953, seeded 1, won 7 matches, *champion* (21–4; games 163–110).
1954, seeded 1, won 4 matches, lost Budge Patty, quarter-final.
1955, seeded 3, won 1 match, lost Gil Shea, 2nd round.
1956, seeded 8, won 5 matches, lost Kenneth Rosewall, semi-final.
1957, seeded 6, won 4 matches, lost Sven Davidson, quarter-final.
1958–1966, did not play.
1967, unseeded, won 1 match, lost Giordane Majoli, 2nd round.
1969, unseeded, won 0 matches, lost Roger Taylor, 1st round.

Matches: 31–8; sets 103–39; games 824–594.

Longest Match: Semi-final 1953, beat Mervyn Rose 6–4 10–12 9–11 6–4 6–3 – a total of 71 games.

Age on winning singles: 29 years 307 days.

Overall Record:

	Titles	Matches		
		Played	Won	Lost
Singles	1	39	31	8
Doubles	0	35	24	11
Mixed	4	29	26	3
Total	5	103	81	22

Career Achievements:
The Championships, Wimbledon: singles 1953; mixed 1953–1956.
US Championships: singles 1954; doubles 1952, 1954; mixed 1953–1955.
French Championships: doubles 1954, 1955; mixed 1953.
Australian Championships: doubles 1955.
Total Grand Slam titles: 15 – singles 2, doubles 5, mixed 8.
Italian Championships: mixed 1953, 1954.
US Davis Cup team: 1951–1957, winning 38 from 55 matches (singles 24–12; doubles 14–5) in 23 ties.

Full name: Elias Victor Seixas
Born: 30th August, 1923, Philadelphia, Pennsylvania, USA.

Jaroslav Drobny

1954

Magic from Bohemia

There was a fairy tale quality about the victory of Jaroslav Drobny in 1954. His success was greeted as if he were a British player – and in a sense he was, for he had an English wife and lived in Sussex. He was a Czech through and through but the upsets of the stormy politics before World War II and in its aftermath contrived to give him the greatest variety of national labels a lawn tennis player ever had.

He first played at Wimbledon in 1938 as a promising 16-year-old lad whose father was the groundsman at a club in Prague. He was, naturally, labelled as from Czechoslovakia. But when he came back in 1939 – when he won two rounds and lost to Britain's Bunny Austin with the not unimpressive score of 5–7 7–9, retired through injury – his identity was 'Bohemia Moravia', that being the rump left after the German aggression. It had been in 1938, incidentally, that the youthful Drobny had taken Don Budge, then in the course of his memorable Grand Slam year, to a full five sets in Prague.

When he returned in 1946, as a Czechoslovak again, he set the meeting upside down by beating the favourite, Jack Kramer, in the fourth round. Kramer had a blistered hand and it was a long, tense affair, Drobny measuring the win 2–6 17–15 6–3 3–6 6–3. Not that it was his longest at Wimbledon by far.

Still as a Czech, Drobny reached the final in 1949. There he led by two sets to one against Ted Schroeder before losing in the fifth. A year later he was labelled as from Egypt. He had become a refugee from his homeland and that nation had offered him a passport. He again reached the final in 1952 and this time he lost to Frank Sedgman.

But if technically Egyptian, Drobny had come to be very British. And it was as a British hero he came through the most remarkable and exciting contest played up to that time in the third round in 1953. His surging, splendid battle against his friend Budge Patty went on for four hours 20 minutes and, after six match balls the other way, brought Drobny victory by 8–6 16–18 3–6 8–6 12–10. Two matches later Drobny, exhausted, lost a little tamely to Kurt Nielsen.

Drobny was seeded 11th in 1954. The selectors' judgment proved much amiss. He beat the second seeded Lew Hoad in the quarter-finals. A round later he beat Patty, this time in four sets. Ken Rosewall was his opponent in the final. Fate was perhaps perverse in this. Drobny, twice a losing finalist at that stage, had acquired the reputation as a man who could not win the big match. Rosewall a great player by any standard, was to suffer the first of four final defeats, the last in 1974, and never did get hold of the title.

Be that as it may, Drobny and Rosewall played one of the finest finals. It extended to four sets only, but with the score of 13–11 4–6 6–2 9–7 to Drobny its 58 games were the highest number played at that stage. Drobny, loved more than ever, last played under his Egyptian label in 1959. In 1960 he played singles for the last time, 22 years after his first appearance. He was then firmly 'GB', having become naturalized at last.

His left-handed touch was magic, especially on clay courts. He twice took the French title and three times the Italian. At Wimbledon in the immediate post-war years his service was among the fastest. A shoulder injury caused him to modify its pace. A special shot of his was the smash. When lobbed on the backhand side he had a knack of contorting his body round to make a normal, and usually deadly, smash.

In 1971, now 49, he entered the mixed doubles one last time with Joyce Williams to extend his memorable span of competition to a remarkable 33 years.

Wimbledon Singles Record:
1938, unseeded, won 0 matches, lost Alejandro Russell, 1st round.
1939, unseeded, won 2 matches, lost Henry Austin, 3rd round.
1946, unseeded, won 5 matches, lost Geoffrey Brown, semi-final.
1947, seeded 6, won 3 matches, lost Budge Patty, quarter-final.
1948, seeded 5, won 1 match, lost Gianni Cucelli, 2nd round.
1949, seeded 6, won 6 matches, lost Ted Schroeder, final.
1950, seeded 3, won 5 matches, lost Frank Sedgman, semi-final.
1951, seeded 2, won 2 matches, lost Anthony Mottram, 3rd round.
1952, seeded 2, won 6 matches, lost Frank Sedgman, final.
1953, seeded 4, won 5 matches, lost Kurt Nielsen, semi-final.
1954, seeded 11, won 7 matches, *champion* (21–2; games 153–95).
1955, seeded 6, won 4 matches, lost Tony Trabert, quarter-final.
1956, seeded 5, won 0 matches, lost Ramanathan Krishnan, 1st round.
1957, unseeded, won 3 matches, lost Ashley Cooper, 2nd round.
1958, unseeded, won 3 matches, lost Mal Anderson, 4th round.
1959, unseeded, won 0 matches, lost Alan Mills, 1st round.
1960, unseeded, won 0 matches, lost Wolfgang Stuck, 1st round.

Matches: 50–16; sets 165–67; games 1,335–1,021.

Longest Match: 3rd round 1953, beat Budge Patty 8–6 16–18 3–6 8–6 12–10 – a total of 93 games.

Age on winning singles: 32 years 263 days.

Overall Record:

	Titles	*Matches*		
		Played	*Won*	*Lost*
Singles	1	66	50	16
Doubles	0	34	26	8
Mixed	0	16	11	5
Total	1	116	87	29

Career Achievements:
The Championships, Wimbledon: singles 1954.
French Championships: singles 1951, 1952; doubles 1948; mixed 1948.
Total Grand Slam titles: 5 – singles 3, doubles 1, mixed 1
Italian Championships: singles 1950, 1951, 1953, doubles 1951, 1952, 1954, 1956
Czechoslovak Davis Cup team: 1946–1949, winning 36 from 43 matches (singles 24–4; doubles 13–2) in 15 ties.

Full name: Jaroslav Drobny
Born: 12th October, 1921, Prague, Czechoslovakia.
Died: 13th September, 2001, Tooting, London, England.

Tony Trabert

1955

Decisive Brevity

Like the hero who gave his name to his birthplace, Cincinnati, Tony Trabert made a brief and brilliant intrusion to the centre of affairs. He established himself at the top when he won the US National singles in 1953 after beating Ken Rosewall in the semi-finals. His dominance endured two years, after which he became a professional. The traditional amateur game saw his heavy pressure and solid backhand no more.

In both 1954 and 1955 he won the French Championship. There was not to be another American winner until the victory of 17-year-old Michael Chang in 1989. These were his only years at Wimbledon. He was the top seed both times.

In 1954 he was engaged in a tremendous 4th round match against the Swede, Sven Davidson. He won 3–6 12–10 6–0 7–9 6–3, a doughty effort. Two matches later, in the semi-finals, the fluent skills of Rosewall routed him severely.

He came back a year later to recoup his losses with a vengeance. He was unstoppable. He arrived in the quarter-finals not having played a set longer than ten games. At that stage Jaroslav Drobny contrived to extend the opening set to 14 games. So did Budge Patty in the semi-finals. The finalist against Trabert was not the expected Rosewall, who had been brought down in the semi-finals by the Dane, Kurt Nielsen. Thus for the second time that diligent and rough hewn player was unseeded and within sight of the title.

But Trabert quenched his ambitions quickly. There was a second set of 12 games, no more pressure than that. Accordingly, Trabert won the singles without having lost a set. At the time the only other man to have done as much since the abolition of the challenge round was Don Budge in 1938. Since Trabert's day two other champions have kept a clean sheet: Chuck McKinley in 1963 and Bjorn Borg in 1976.

Nor, a little later, did he lose a set in winning his US title, any more than in taking it for the first time in 1953. Only one other man in history has won the Wimbledon and US singles in the one year without losing a set – and that was

Laurie Doherty in 1903 when he had only the Challenge Round to play at Wimbledon.

It could be that no champion has been so underestimated as the indomitable Trabert.

Wimbledon Singles Record:
1950, unseeded, won 1 match, lost
    Anthony Mottram, 2nd round.
1951–1953, did not play.
1954, seeded 1, won 5 matches, lost
    Kenneth Rosewall, semi-final.
1955, seeded 1, won 7 matches,
    champion (21–0; games 131–60).

Matches: 13–2; sets 41–8; games
    287–182.

Longest Match: 4th round 1954, beat
    Sven Davidson 3–6 12–10 6–0 7–9
    6–3 – a total of 62 games.

Age on winning singles: 24 years 319
    days.

Overall Record:

	Titles	Matches Played	Won	Lost
Singles	1	15	13	2
Doubles	0	16	13	3
Mixed	0	0	0	0
Total	1	31	26	5

Career Achievements:
The Championships, Wimbledon: singles 1955.
US Championships: singles 1953, 1955; doubles 1954.
French Championships: singles 1954, 1955; doubles 1950, 1954, 1955.
Australian Championships: doubles 1955.
Total Grand Slam titles: 10 – singles 5, doubles 5
Italian Championships: doubles 1950.
US Davis Cup team: 1951–1955, winning 27 from 35 matches (singles 16–5; doubles 11–3)
    in 14 ties.

Full name: Marion Anthony (Tony) Trabert
Born: 16th August, 1930, Cincinnati, Ohio, USA.

Lew Hoad

1956, 1957

Dynamic Australian

Lew Hoad was born in New South Wales in the same month as Ken Rosewall and they were junior rivals. It was as partners when 17-year-olds in 1952 that they astonished the lawn tennis world by reaching the semi-finals of the doubles in the major championships. Until the end of 1956 not the least interest of the international game was their progress as a pair and their conflict as rivals.

Whether it worked out better for Hoad or Rosewall is a matter of opinion. Rosewall never won the Wimbledon singles, Hoad did it twice. Furthermore Hoad came within one match of winning the Grand Slam. Had he won the US singles in 1956 he would have done so. He lost the final – to Rosewall. But if Rosewall never won Wimbledon his lighter frame and more gentle craft gave him unusually long life as a player.

Hoad in contrast was unable to resume in the open game where he had left off as an amateur. A strained back was the cause. Yet in his prime his iron wrist and brawny muscle combined to make him a dynamic powerhouse of a player. When at his peak, as he was in beating Ashley Cooper to take his second Wimbledon singles in 1957, one could not resist the conclusion that no other man in the game, however great, could have lived against him.

In his amateur career he never fell short of the fourth round at Wimbledon. He reached that stage as a 17-year-old in 1952, when Jaroslav Drobny, the two-time French champion, beat him. In the next three years he fell in the quarter-finals, to Vic Seixas, Drobny again, and Budge Patty. Only those of championship calibre beat him.

Hoad was top seed in 1956 and Mal Anderson, from Queensland, gave him a difficult quarter-final. Hoad lost the first set and won the fourth 13–11. His stable mate Rosewall was his final victim. Power conquered finesse though only in four sets. Rosewall's revenge came in the US final later.

In the course of 1957 Hoad failed to retain his Australian and French titles. At Wimbledon he conceded a set only in the quarter-finals to his fellow Australian, Mervyn Rose. In the last match Cooper won only five games in all and must have reckoned himself fortunate to get as many.

That was Hoad's last match as an amateur. At the LTA Ball where his triumph was celebrated he affirmed he would be back to defend his title the following year. It transpired that he felt it would have been ungracious to say otherwise, for the next day he flew to New York and within twenty-four hours had signed as a professional for what was then a record guarantee of $30,000. Rosewall had left amateurism at the start of the year.

Like Bjorn Borg a generation later, Hoad never won the US singles. He was an uneven player in that here and there he seemed bored and ready to lose to men below his class. That was a quirk of genius. When he was inspired to be at his most dynamic he would have beaten anybody.

He settled in Spain as a teaching professional in due course, with a club of his own and died tragically of leukaemia long before his time in 1994 at the age of 59.

Wimbledon Singles Record:

1952, unseeded, won 3 matches, lost Jaroslav Drobny, 4th round.
1953, seeded 6, won 4 matches, lost Victor Seixas, quarter-final.
1954, seeded 2, won 4 matches, lost Jaroslav Drobny, quarter-final.
1955, seeded 4, won 4 matches, lost Budge Patty, quarter-final.
1956, seeded 1, won 7 matches, *champion* (sets 21–2; games 152–90).
1957, seeded 1, won 7 matches, *champion* (sets 21–1; games 138–79).

1958–1967, did not play.

1968, seeded 7, won 2 matches, lost Robert Hewitt, 3rd round.

1969, did not play.

1970, unseeded, won 1 match, lost Ismail El Shafei, 2nd round.

1971, did not play.

1972, unseeded, won 0 matches, lost Jurgen Fassbender, 1st round.

Matches: 32–7; sets 104–31; games 784–531.

Longest Match: 3rd round 1968, lost Robert Hewitt 3–6 11–9 6–1 3–6 6–3 – a total of 54 games.

Age on first winning singles: 21 years 226 days.

Age on last winning singles: 22 years 224 days.

Overall Record:

	Titles	Matches Played	Won	Lost
Singles	2	39	32	7
Doubles	3	44	36	8
Mixed	0	19	15	4
Total	5	102	83	19

Career Achievements:

The Championships, Wimbledon: singles 1956, 1957; doubles 1953, 1955, 1956.

US Championships: doubles 1956.

French Championships: singles 1956; doubles 1953; mixed 1954.

Australian Championships: singles 1956; doubles 1953, 1956, 1957.

Total Grand Slam titles: 13 – singles 4, doubles 8, mixed 1.

Italian Championships: singles 1956; doubles 1953, 1956, 1957.

Australian Davis Cup team: 1953–1956, winning 17 from 21 matches (singles 10–2; doubles 7–2) in 9 ties.

Full name: Lewis Alan (Lew) Hoad

Born: 23rd November 1934, Glebe, NSW, Australia.

Died: 3rd July 1994, Fuengirola, Spain.

Ashley Cooper

1958

Achievement Deferred

When Ashley Cooper came from Melbourne to compete at Wimbledon for the first time he did well for a 17-year-old. Among others he beat the Queenslander Roy Emerson, two months younger, and yielded only in the round of 16 to Ken Rosewall. It was a heartening beginning.

In 1955, when he was 18, he endured greater hardships. He lost his opening match to Mervyn Rose, the Australian left-hander. More traumatic perhaps was 1956 when the rewards of better performance were taken away. He survived three very long, five set matches, the second of which was against the Swede, Sven Davidson, the number three seed. Having come through the toils of 15 sets he fell in the 20th. This last five setter was against the little known Allen Morris from Georgia. The latter became a surprise quarter-finalist and Cooper departed having played a total of 200 games.

By 1957 he came with the kudos of having won the Australian singles. With his dogged efficiency he hauled himself to the final, being pressed only in a four set semi-final against Neale Fraser, whom he had beaten for the Australian crown. But in the Wimbledon final Cooper met Lew Hoad, then at the peak of his powers. Hoad produced a major *tour de force* and Cooper was routed.

In 1958, by which time Hoad was in the professional ranks, Cooper had the field left clear. He was again the champion of Australia. Nonetheless he had to struggle, notably in the fourth round against the heavy left-handed serving of South Africa's Abe Segal. There were four sets to this but the first was of 24 games and the last 26. Five sets followed in the quarters against the British Bobby Wilson with a four-setter against Rose before his final victory against Fraser, which he clinched in a 13–11 fourth set.

Cooper continued to ride the crest of the wave in the United States. He took the American crown as well and signed the professional contract then being offered to the champions as a matter of course. He was only just 22 years old. His young brother, John Cooper, later came on to the Wimbledon scene and was a doubles finalist with Fraser in 1973.

Wimbledon Singles Record:

1954, unseeded, won 3 matches, lost Kenneth Rosewall, 4th round.
1955, unseeded, won 0 matches, lost Mervyn Rose, 1st round.
1956, unseeded, won 3 matches, lost Allen Morris, 4th round.
1957, seeded 2, won 6 matches, lost Lewis Hoad, final.
1958, seeded 1, won 7 matches, *champion* (sets 21–7; games 182–140).

Matches: 19–4; sets 60–26; games 508–399.

Longest Match: 3rd round 1958, beat Abe Segal 13–11 6–3 3–6 14–12 – a total of 68 games.

Age on winning singles: 21 years 292 days.

Overall Record:

	Titles	Matches		
		Played	*Won*	*Lost*
Singles	1	23	19	4
Doubles	0	18	13	5
Mixed	0	3	1	2
Total	1	44	33	11

Career Achievements:

The Championships, Wimbledon: singles 1958.
US Championships: singles 1958; doubles 1957.
French Championships: doubles 1957, 1958.
Australian Championships: singles 1957, 1958; doubles 1958.
Total Grand Slam titles: 8 – singles 4, doubles 4.
Australian Davis Cup team: 1957–1958, winning 2 from 4 matches (singles 2–2) in 2 ties.

Full name: Ashley John Cooper
Born: 15th September 1936, Melbourne, Australia.

Alex Olmedo

1959

The Man from Peru

The first South American with Indian blood to hoist himself to the top flights of the game was probably Francisco Segura, whose double-handed skills reverberated through-out the game in the immediate post World War II years. He was from Ecuador. He won the Queen's Club tournament in 1946 but had become a professional by the end of 1947 without displaying his highest talents.

From Peru came Alex Olmedo and, like Segura, he learned his lawn tennis as a student in the US where his college chums dubbed him 'The Chief', a nickname which stuck. Olmedo, indeed, became a thoroughgoing Californian. In due course his Davis Cup loyalties were American. He was a lively, athletic player. It looked as if he would go on getting better as his game matured but the strains of the professional career which he adopted perhaps suited him less than others. He made a brilliant start and beat Pancho Gonzales but achieved not much more.

Olmedo made no impression at his first attempt at Wimbledon in 1957 when he was 21. He did not return until 1959. He was top seeded, for at the start of the year not only had he won the Australian championship but also both his singles for the US in the Challenge Round of the Davis Cup as a makeweight.

His high form persisted at Wimbledon. The Indian, Ramanathan Krishnan, took a set from him. So did the Chilean, Luis Ayala. In the semi-finals he beat Roy Emerson straightforwardly and he was hardly less forthright in the title match itself against Rod Laver. With hindsight it could be seen that his final scalp was the most distinguished.

He nearly made a double of it. In the US Championship Olmedo looked a winner until the final where Neale Fraser served too well for him.

He returned to the open Wimbledon but after eight years was rusty at those keen levels. He won two rounds in 1968 when Emerson avenged his loss of 1959. A year later in Wimbledon's first round, Ron Homberg avenged his loss at the 1959 Forest Hills meeting.

Peruvian history or not he was the first player in history to win in the Challenge Round three live Davis Cup matches, two singles and a doubles, for the USA. Stan Smith was the next to do so in the Final Round of 1972 and John McEnroe repeated the feat in 1981.

Wimbledon Singles Record:
1957, unseeded, won 0 matches, lost Mervyn Rose, 1st round.
1958, did not play.
1959, seeded 1, won 7 matches, *champion* (sets 21–2; games 134–77).
1960–1967 did not play.
1968, unseeded, won 2 matches lost Roy Emerson, 3rd round.
1969, unseeded, won 0 matches, lost Ron Holmberg, 1st round.
1970, 1971, did not play.
1972, unseeded, won 1 match, lost Ian Fletcher, 2nd round.

Matches: 10–4; sets 34–16; games 274–224.

Longest Match: 1st round 1969, lost Ron Holmberg 6–8 6–4 4–6 6–2 5–7 – a total of 54 games.

Age on winning singles: 23 years 101 days.

Overall Record:

	Titles	Matches Played	Won	Lost
Singles	1	14	10	4
Doubles	0	10	5	5
Mixed	0	0	0	0
Total	1	24	15	9

Career Achievements:
The Championships, Wimbledon: singles 1959.
US Championships: doubles 1958.
Australian Championships: singles 1959.
Total Grand Slam titles: 3 – singles 2, doubles 1.
US Davis Cup team: 1958–1959, winning 7 from 9 matches (singles 5–1; doubles 2–1) in 3 ties.

Full name: Alejandro Rodriguez Olmedo
Born: 24th March 1936, Arequipa, Peru.

Neale Fraser

1960

Service to Remember

This Australian left-hander was a champion to remember on more than one count. His opponents will remember him most for his service. It had all the punishing bite of which the southpaw is capable, plus more. Not only could he make the ball break in killing measure wide to the right-hander's backhand from the left court but he had a 'googly' which, used sparingly, confounded his opponents utterly in the right court

Without his deadly service Fraser, a most popular fellow, could hardly have hoped to be a champion. Another count on which to remember his success was its achievement after being six times match point down in the quarter-final. It was a remarkable contest against the American Earl 'Butch' Buchholz. Fraser lost the first and third sets and as the fourth went on and on it was Buchholz who threatened victory. But the American began to suffer the spasms of cramp. When the score was 15 games all he collapsed on court for the second time. The referee had no choice but to order his retirement.

After this escape Fraser easily beat the Indian, Ramanathan Krishnan. In the final he beat Rod Laver, who was there for the second year. At that time Laver, *vis-à-vis* Fraser, was a youngster facing a mentor. Fraser got the title.

That was his seventh Wimbledon visit. A year later, when seeded one, he yielded to the Britain's Bobby Wilson in the last sixteen. A year later he went further, but only to the semi-finals where Laver, now with one championship behind him, gave short shrift.

Nonetheless 1962 was a remarkable year in that not only was Neale Fraser in the last four of the singles but so too was Dr John Fraser, his brother. A medical doctor, he was hardly a serious performer; but he had tagged along with his famous sibling and had enjoyed uninhibited success until Martin Mulligan beat him. The last occasion when two brothers were still surviving at that stage of the event was with Reggie and Laurie Doherty in 1898. The Fraser brothers were also in the last four of the doubles, but with different partners, Neale with Roy Emerson and John with Laver.

It was in 1962, too, that Neale won the mixed doubles. He did so with the American veteran Margaret du Pont. He was 28. She was over 44 years old and no one more senior, man or woman, had achieved as much until Martina Navratilova, playing with India's Leander Paes, became the mixed doubles champion in 2003, at the age of 46.

Wimbledon Singles Record:
1954, unseeded, won 1 match, lost Mervyn Rose, 2nd round.
1955, unseeded, won 0 matches, lost Hugh Stewart, 1st round (won plate).
1956, unseeded, won 4 matches, lost Hamilton Richardson, quarter-final.
1957, seeded 5, won 5 matches, lost Ashley Cooper, semi-final.
1958, seeded 4, won 6 matches, lost Ashley Cooper, final.
1959, seeded 2, won 4 matches, lost Barry MacKay, quarter-final.
1960, seeded 1, won 7 matches, *champion* (sets 20–4; games 150–95).
1961, seeded 1, won 3 matches, lost Bobby Wilson, 4th round.

1962, seeded 3, won 5 matches, lost Rodney Laver, semi-final.
1963, 1964 did not play.
1965, unseeded, won 2 matches, lost Robert Hewitt, 3rd round.
1966–1971, did not play.
1972, unseeded, won 0 matches, lost Adriano Panatta, 1st round.
1973, unseeded, won 0 matches, lost Chico Hagley, 1st round.
1974, unseeded, won 1 match, lost Jeff Borowiak, 2nd round.
1975, unseeded, won 0 matches, lost Onny Parun, 1st round.

Matches: 38–13; sets 122–65; games 1,111–899.

Longest Match: 4th round 1959, beat Olando Sirola 3–6 6–3 14–12 8–10 6–3 – a total of 71 games.

Age on winning singles: 26 years 272 days.

Overall Record:

| | Titles | Matches | | |
		Played	Won	Lost
Singles	1	51	38	13
Doubles	2	63	50	13
Mixed	1	50	37	13
Total	4	164	125	39

Career Achievements:
The Championships, Wimbledon: singles 1960; doubles 1959, 1961; mixed 1962.
US Championships: singles 1959, 1960; doubles 1957, 1959, 1960; mixed 1958–1960.
French Championships: doubles 1958, 1960, 1962.
Australian Championships: doubles 1957, 1958, 1962; mixed 1956.
Total Grand Slam titles: 19 – singles 3, doubles 11, mixed 5.
Italian Championships: doubles 1957, 1959, 1961, 1962
Australian Davis Cup team: 1958–1963, winning 18 from 21 matches (singles 11–1; doubles 7–2) in 11 ties.

Full name: Neale Andrew Fraser
Born: 3rd October, 1933, St. Kilda, Melbourne, Australia.

Rod Laver

1961, 1962, 1968, 1969

Persistent Genius

In 1961, the Queenslander Rod Laver, red-headed, left-handed and known universally as 'The Rockhampton Rocket' became the singles champion for the first time. In 1960 he had lost in the final to his fellow Australian left-hander, Neale Fraser. His next defeat in the singles at Wimbledon was in 1970 when the British No.1 Roger Taylor beat him in the fourth round. He was 31 years old.

This spell of invincibility had a five years interregnum so far as The Championships were concerned, for Laver became a professional at the end of 1962 and was unable to compete again until the onset of open tennis in 1968. Nonetheless he did win a professional event that was staged on the Centre Court in the late summer of 1967. For virtually a decade Laver was without a peer.

Yet when he made his first appearance at Wimbledon in 1956 his genius, though not his promise, was not all that evident. He came when he was 17 and played in the junior event. The American Ron Holmberg beat him 6–1 6–1 in the final. He also competed in The Championships proper. The big Italian Orlando Sirola beat him 7–5 6–4 6–2 in the first round.

Laver's next challenge was in 1958 when he was 19. He won two rounds. A year later he was a force to reckon with. He won a hectic semi-final against the big-serving American, Barry MacKay. The score was 11–13 11–9 10–8 7–9 6–3. Having survived that tough one he lost the final fairly easily to Alex Olmedo, the man from Peru. He was unseeded.

The next year also he was the losing finalist, this time to Fraser. In 1961 he was the champion. And again in 1962. Then, when he was allowed back, he celebrated the liberation of the game by winning the first open Wimbledon in 1968. He took what was in effect his fourth successive singles in 1969.

All records for consistent success fell to him thereby. Perry had had 21 sequential singles victories. Laver had had 31 before he lost in 1970. He won the first three of his finals in straight sets. Only in 1969, when he beat John Newcombe, was he taken to four.

His last real Wimbledon effort was in 1971 when he yielded in the quarter-finals to the American Tom Gorman. It ranked as the best win the man from Seattle ever had. There was a welcome re-appearance in 1977 but that was to grace the Centenary Celebrations. He had a win nonetheless. He was then 36.

Outside the context of Wimbledon his achievements went to new limits. He twice won the Grand Slam, for the second time in 1969.

His first achievement at that exalted level was in 1962. One must make the qualification that at that time many of the leading men were non-combatants in the traditional events, because they were professionals. Nonetheless Laver's perform-ance was stupefying in its grandeur.

He took not only the Grand Slam but two other major championships as well. His run of triumph in singles that year comprised, to list them as he won them, the championships of Australia, Italy, France, Wimbledon, Germany and the USA. At one stage he was within one point of not making that unique record. In the French quarter-finals against Martin Mulligan, a fellow Australian (albeit destined to have Italian Davis Cup loyalty in 1968), he saved a match point in the fourth set.

Laver played for Australia in five Challenge (or Final) Rounds of the Davis Cup. He lost his debut singles in 1959, he won two singles in 1960, 1961, 1962 and, having been called back for service in 1973, another two when he was 35 years old.

Laver had everything a player could have. His backhand, played sweepingly with top spin, was as deadly a left-hander's shot that ever was. 'The Rocket' was a brilliant genius and a delight to watch.

Wimbledon Singles Record:
1956, unseeded, won 0 matches, lost Olando Sirola, 1st round.
1957, did not play.
1958, unseeded, won 2 matches, lost Jaroslav Drobny, 2nd round.
1959, unseeded, won 6 matches, lost Alex Olmedo, final.
1960, seeded 3, won 6 matches, lost Neale Fraser, final.
1961, seeded 2, won 7 matches, *champion* (sets 21–4; games 148–88).
1962, seeded 1, won 7 matches, *champion* (sets 21–1; games 156–84).
1963–1967, did not play.
1968, seeded 1, won 7 matches, *champion* (sets 21–5; games 151–97).
1969, seeded 1, won 7 matches, *champion* (sets 21–6; games 153–96).
1970, seeded 1, won 3 matches, lost Roger Taylor, 4th round.
1971, seeded 1, won 4 matches, lost Tom Gorman, quarter-final.
1972–1976, did not play.
1977, unseeded, won 1 match, lost Richard Stockton, 2nd round.

Matches: 50–7; sets 153–50; games 1,197–811.

Longest Match: Semi-final 1959, beat Barry MacKay 11–13 11–9 10–8 7–9 6–3 – a total of 87 games.

Age on first winning singles: 22 years 332 days.

Age on last winning singles: 30 years 330 days.

Overall Record:

	Titles	Matches		
		Played	Won	Lost
Singles	4	57	50	7
Doubles	1	43	33	10
Mixed	2	17	15	2
Total	7	117	98	19

Career Achievements:

The Championships, Wimbledon: singles 1961, 1962, 1968, 1969; doubles 1971; mixed 1959, 1960.

US Championships: singles 1962, 1969.

French Championships: singles 1962, 1969; doubles 1961; mixed 1961.

Australian Championships: singles 1960, 1962, 1969; doubles 1959–1961, 1969.

Total Grand Slam titles: 20 – singles 11, doubles 6, mixed 3. Uniquely twice a 'Grand Slam' winner in 1962 and 1969.

Italian Championships: singles 1962, 1971; doubles 1962.

Australian Davis Cup team: 1959–1962, winning 20 from 24 matches (singles 16–4; doubles 4–0) in 11 ties.

Won: 47 singles titles, 37 doubles titles

Played: 491 singles, winning 392 (Open Era)

Prize money: $1,564,213

Full name: Rodney George Laver
Born: 9th August 1938, Rockhampton, Queensland, Australia.

Charles McKinley

1963

No Seeds, No Sets

Charles Robert McKinley, from St Louis, thrived more at Wimbledon than in his own US Nationals, where he never got beyond the singles semifinals; albeit he was thrice a doubles winner there with Dennis Ralston. At Wimbledon he made his mark at his second visit in 1961 when he went all the way to the singles final before losing to Rod Laver.

In 1963 he made himself the successor to that great Australian following Laver's switch to the professional ranks. He had the status as the number four seed and his victory was unique.

It happened that 1963 was a very wet year, with the timetable at sixes and sevens. The seeding list was widely criticised from the start. Its imperfections were probably the outcome of the appointment that year of a new referee, Mike Gibson. As a 'new boy' he was given less of his head than was normal with the seeding. The list bore all the marks of woolly committee decisions.

Be that as it may, events fell to propel McKinley forward in a way that had not happened since seeding was introduced in 1927. In the quarter-finals McKinley should have played, according to the seeding, the Australian Martin Mulligan; but Mulligan's delicacy of touch was outshone in the fourth round and McKinley played, and beat Britain's Bobby Wilson instead. Roy Emerson was cast as the semi-finalist. That mercurial Australian yielded in the round before to the German Wilhelm Bungert, not seeded. In the final McKinley should have played the second seed, Manuel Santana of Spain. But Santana had fallen one round earlier to the Australian Fred Stolle, not a seed.

Accordingly 'Chuck' McKinley became champion without having played a seeded man. Nor did he lose a set in any match. No seeds, no sets. McKinley stands on his own.

He was athletic to a high degree, almost acrobatic in his energetic volleying. He gave valiant Davis Cup service to the US and by taking the fifth and decisive singles against John Newcombe won the trophy for them in 1964. A year later he was worsted by Roy Emerson in the same vital match.

At the Wimbledon Ball McKinley had another unique experience. There was no woman champion with whom to open the dancing, for rain had delayed that final until the Monday, so he paired with his wife instead.

Unusually for the champions of that time, McKinley never turned professional, preferring instead to pursue a business career. Sadly it was a short career. In 1986, after a short spell in hospital, McKinley died of a brain tumor at the age of 45.

Wimbledon Singles Record:
1960, unseeded, won 1 match, lost Pierre Darmon, 2nd round.
1961, seeded 8, won 6 matches, lost Rodney Laver, Final.
1962, seeded 5, won 1 match, lost Michael Hann, 2nd round.
1963, seeded 4, won 7 matches, *champion* (sets 21–0; games 140–82).
1964, seeded 2, won 5 matches, lost Fred Stolle, semi-final.

Matches: 20–4; sets 63–21; games 477–349.

Longest Match: Semi-final 1964, lost to Fred Stolle 6–4 8–10 7–9 4–6 – a total of 54 games.

Age on winning singles: 22 years 181 days.

Overall Record:

	Titles	Matches Played	Won	Lost
Singles	1	24	20	4
Doubles	0	17	13	4
Mixed	0	0	0	0
Total	1	41	33	8

Career Achievements:
The Championships, Wimbledon: singles 1963.
US Championships: doubles 1961, 1963, 1964.
Total Grand Slam titles: 4 – singles 1, doubles 3.
US Davis Cup team: 1960–1965, winning 29 from 38 matches (singles 16–6; doubles 13–3) in 16 ties.

Full name: Charles Robert (Chuck) McKinley
Born: 5th January, 1941, St. Louis, Missouri, USA.
Died: 11th August, 1986, Dallas, Texas, USA.

Roy Emerson

1964, 1965

Perpetual Motion

Roy Emerson, a Queenslander from the small country town of Blackbutt, was nothing if not athletic. As a schoolboy of 14 he ran 100 yards in 10.6 second and long jumped 21 feet 6 inches. It is arguable that his prowess marked a turning point in lawn tennis akin to the 4 minute mile of Roger Bannister in athletics. It had been taken for granted over the years that the serve volleyer needed to conserve his energies to go beyond three sets. Emerson by his example proved it could be done for five full sets for match after match, never 'resting' for a set.

He won the Wimbledon singles twice. Like his predecessor, Chuck McKinley, he would probably not have done so had not an even greater Queenslander, Rod Laver, left the amateur ranks. Emerson's first win was at his ninth attempt. In 1965 he won again and in both finals he beat his fellow Australian Fred Stolle, who thus unwillingly equalled the record of the German Gottfried von Cramm in losing three finals running.

That Emerson would have won for the third time in 1966 is overwhelmingly probable. His sharpness and expertise stood on its own. But in the quarter-finals against yet another Australian, the left-handed Owen Davidson, he was over zealous in chasing a drop shot. He hurt himself colliding violently with the net post and, semi-crippled, was beaten. He went on playing at Wimbledon until 1971 when, aged 35, he competed in the singles for the 16th time.

On every surface and in every championship Emerson was a champion of the highest quality. He won the US singles twice and the French Championship twice. His own Australian singles title he won six times. He had doubles titles galore, including a run of six unbeaten years in the French meeting with five different partners.

His tally of Grand Slam titles comes to: singles 12, doubles 16, mixed doubles 1.

His standard of performance in the Davis Cup for Australia was among the finest in that demanding competition where he played in the Challenge Round every year from 1959 to 1967, nine times in all. His record of live singles was nine

won out of nine. His only live match defeats were two losses in his six doubles. His most memorable result was beating the American Chuck McKinley in Cleveland in 1964 by 3–6 6–2 6–4 6–4 in the fifth and decisive match. He had the satisfaction of hitting the ball that actually gave the trophy to Australia on five occasions.

If Emerson stands high in any list of all time greats he also stands high in any roll of outstanding sportsmen if that quality be judged by generosity of spirit. His mercurial talents were awesome and every time he played he enhanced the prestige of the sport.

He was though, a relatively late developer. When he won his first Grand Slam singles titles, the Australian and American in 1961, he was in his 25th year. He began when he was eight and had his first coaching when eleven.

Wimbledon Singles Record:
1954, unseeded, won 1 match, lost Ashley Cooper, 2nd round.
1955, did not play.

1956, unseeded, won 2 matches, lost Robert Howe, 3rd round.

1957, unseeded, won 3 matches, lost Lewis Hoad, 4th round.

1958, did not play.

1959, seeded 8, won 5 matches, lost Alex Olmedo, semi-final.

1960, seeded 6, won 4 matches, lost Rodney Laver, quarter-final.

1961, seeded 4, won 4 matches, lost Ramanathan Krishnan, quarter-final.

1962, seeded 2, won 3 matches, lost Martin. Mulligan, 4th round.

1963, seeded 1, won 4 matches, lost Wilhelm Bungert, quarter-final.

1964, seeded 1, won 7 matches, *champion* (sets 21–2; games 154–93).

1965, seeded 1, won 7 matches, *champion* (sets 21–3; games 151–90).

1966, seeded 1, won 4 matches, lost Owen Davidson, quarter-final.

1967, seeded 2, won 3 matches, lost Nicki Pilic, 4th round.

1968, seeded 5, won 3 matches, lost Thomas Okker, 4th round.

1969, seeded 9, won 3 matches, lost Clifford Drysdale, 4th round.

1970, seeded 10, won 4 matches, lost John Newcombe, quarter-final.

1971, unseeded, won 3 matches, lost Stanley Smith, 4th round.

Matches: 60–14; sets 193–62; games 1,480–1,004.

Longest Match: 2nd round 1962, beat Wilhelm Bungert 13–15 4–6 6–3 6–0 6–4 – a total of 63 games.

Age on first winning singles: 27 years 243 days.

Age on last winning singles: 28 years 241 days.

Overall Record:

	Titles	Matches Played	Won	Lost
Singles	2	74	60	14
Doubles	3	72	60	12
Mixed	0	14	10	4
Total	5	160	130	30

Career Achievements:

The Championships, Wimbledon: singles 1964, 1965; doubles 1959, 1961, 1971.
US Championships: singles 1961, 1964; doubles 1959, 1960, 1965, 1966.
French Championships: singles 1963, 1967; doubles 1960–1965.
Australian Championships: singles 1961, 1963–1967; doubles 1962, 1966, 1969.
Total Grand Slam titles: 28 – singles 12, doubles 16.
Italian Championships: doubles 1959, 1961, 1966: mixed 1961.
Australian Davis Cup team: 1959–1967, winning 34 from 38 matches (singles 21–2; doubles 13–2) in 18 ties.

Full name: Roy Stanley Emerson
Born: 3rd November, 1936, Blackbutt, Queensland, Australia.

Manuel Santana

1966

Gentleman and Artist

Manuel Santana, the champion of 1966, was arguably one of the three greatest touch players in the history of the game – the other two being Henri Cochet of France and Ilie Nastase of Romania – and he was certainly the greatest exponent from Spain. Yet his magic touch, which gave the ability to produce shots apparently defying the laws of physics, was the outcome of a tennis upbringing on slow, clay courts.

His first successes in the top flight were in the French Championships in Paris. When he won for the first time in 1961 it was against Nicola Pietrangeli and he recovered from a deficit of one set to two to prevent the Italian from winning for the third time. Santana was so moved that he could only climb under the net and burst into tears in consolation of his disappointed opponent. He won again in 1964 when he again beat Pietrangeli in the final.

All that was the logical outcome of his superb delicacy of touch and ability to come back from behind on his own surface. He belonged to the school of players, who, having been successful enough to make a joke at their host's expense, said, 'Well, of course, grass is only fit for cows'. Santana said just that when he won the Wimbledon crown in 1966.

His success there, however, had been preceded by an exploit on grass which made it less surprising. He won the US National title at Forest Hills in 1965 when that championship was still being played on turf.

The Wimbledon door was opened for Santana when the Australian Roy Emerson, who seemed overwhelmingly likely to win for the third year, injured himself and was out of contention. He had two very difficult matches before the last, twice being taken to 7–5 in the fifth set by Ken Fletcher and Owen Davidson, Australians both, in the quarter and semi-finals.

He won with greater ease in the final against his American opponent, Dennis Ralston. As a display of generous sportsmanship by both, that contest ranks

amongst the finest. At the change overs they appeared to be congratulating each other on their prowess and as Santana gratefully accepted Ralston's proffered 'coke' he seemed to say that when he got to Spain Ralston should taste his sherry.

An immensely popular winner, Santana was 28 years old and playing for the eighth time. But for his success the year before in New York one would have suspected he was surprised by his own triumph. When he returned to defend his title in 1967 he again surprised everyone.

He lost in the first round. Beginning, as tradition has it, on the Centre Court on the first Monday, he yielded, in four hard fought but ineffective sets, to the American Charles Pasarell.

Santana thus has two distinctions. He is the only Spaniard to have won the men's singles, and he is the only champion to have lost in the opening match of the following year.

Wimbledon Singles Record:

1958, unseeded, won 0 matches, lost Pato Alvarez, 1st round.

1959, unseeded, won 2 matches, lost Olando Sirola, 3rd round.

1960, unseeded, won 24 matches, lost Rodney Laver, 3rd round.

1961, seeded 5, won 1 match, lost Abe Segal, 2nd round.

1962, seeded 6, won 4 matches, lost Rodney Laver, quarter-final.

1963, seeded 2, won 5 matches, lost Fred Stolle, semi-final.

1964, seeded 3, won 3 matches, lost Christian Kuhnke, 4th round.

1965, did not play.

1966, seeded 4, won 7 matches, *champion* (sets 19–5; games 141–98).

1967, seeded 1, won 0 matches, lost Charles Pasarell, 1st round.

1968, seeded 6, won 2 matches, lost Clark Graebner, 3rd round.

Matches: 26–9; sets 81–45; games 723–582.

Longest Match: 2nd round 1960, beat Alan Lane 6–3 5–7 10–12 6–4 8–6 – a total of 67 games.

Age on winning singles: 28 years 52 days.

Overall Record:

	Titles	*Matches*		
		Played	*Won*	*Lost*
Singles	1	35	26	9
Doubles	0	26	18	8
Mixed	0	0	0	0
Total	1	61	44	17

Career Achievements:

The Championships, Wimbledon: singles 1966.

US Championships: singles 1965.

French Championships: singles 1961, 1964; doubles 1963.

Total Grand Slam titles: 5 – singles 4, doubles 1.

Spanish Davis Cup team: 1958–1973, winning 92 from 120 matches (singles 69–17; doubles 23–11) in 46 ties.

Full name: Manuel Martinez Santana
Born: 10th May, 1938, Madrid, Spain.

John Newcombe

1967, 1970, 1971

Amateur and Open Champion

Like another famous Australian, Rod Laver, John Newcombe won the singles at both an amateur and open Wimbledon. Had not politics intruded Newcombe might also have equalled Laver's feat of winning the title four times in all.

In 1972, having already won in both the preceding years, he would have been a strong favourite. It happened that year there was a pointless – as it can now be seen to have been – wrangle about players under contract and the authority of the International Tennis Federation. Because of this, Newcombe was barred from competing. He would also have been among the front runners one year later, 1973, but that was the year of the boycott by the Association of Tennis Professionals and Newcombe was again an absentee.

When at last Newcombe got back in 1974 he was 30 years old. He was seeded one, but, in a cold wind, was worsted by the 39-year-old Ken Rosewall in the quarter-finals. But two prime chances had passed him by and one may note that in 1973 he was sharp enough to take the US singles for the second time, six years after his first success.

Newcombe was one of the game's heavyweights, a resolute serve and volley man who rode out many a storm by the consistency of his attacking pressure. He came to his peak rather late. He won his first Wimbledon singles in 1967 before turning professional with WCT's 'Handsome Eight'. He was 23 and had been at Wimbledon six times before.

His potential had been seen early in Australia and there was the suspicion that he had been given too much responsibility too early. His first Davis Cup experience was in 1963, when he was 19. There was no warm-up for him. He lost to both Dennis Ralston and, in the fifth and deciding match, to Chuck McKinley. He was not given singles responsibility in the Challenge Round again until 1967.

If his progress towards greatness was slow it was the surer for it. He was never taken beyond four sets in his first Wimbledon win in 1967 and the final against the unseeded German, Wilhelm Bungert, was among the easiest ever.

Arthur Ashe, destined to be champion seven years later, thwarted him in the fourth round of the first open Wimbledon in 1968. The year following he came within one match of his second title; instead Laver won his fourth. In 1970 he had a tremendous quarter-final tussle against Roy Emerson, surviving in the 20th game of the fifth set. He went on to win the final against Ken Rosewall in another full length contest. His third singles win came in 1971 when the last match was again five sets, this against the American Stan Smith, the next champion-to-be and cast in much the same heavyweight mould as Newcombe.

Thus Newcombe made himself a three times singles champion at his 11th appearance. He last played in singles, for the 14th time, in 1978.

A giant in singles he was even more successful in doubles, most notably with the left-handed Tony Roche; he took five of six Wimbledon championships with him. Their final win in 1968, the first open meeting, against Rosewall and Fred Stolle, comprised 70 games (3–6 8–6 5–7 14–12 6–3) and none longer, in number of games, was ever played.

A doughty stalwart, Newcombe was a professional to his fingertips and one who never failed to enhance the image of lawn tennis.

Wimbledon Singles Record:

1961, unseeded, won 0 matches, lost Jan-Erik Lundquist, 1st round.

1962, unseeded, won 1 match, lost Rafael Osuna, 2nd round.

1963, unseeded, won 0 matches, lost John Hillebrand, 1st round.

1964, unseeded, won 0 matches, lost Fred Stolle, 1st round.

1965, seeded 6, won 3 matches, lost Clifford Drysdale, 4th round.

1966, seeded 5, won 2 matches, lost Kenneth Fletcher, 3rd round.

1967, seeded 3, won 7 matches, *champion* (sets 21–2; games 152–97).

1968, seeded 4, won 3 matches, lost Arthur Ashe, 4th round.

1969, seeded 6, won 6 matches, lost Rodney Laver, final.

1970, seeded 2 won 7 matches, *champion* (sets 21–4; games 164–103).

1971, seeded 2, won 7 matches, *champion* (sets 21–3; games 142–90).

1972, 1973, did not play.

1974, seeded 1, won 4 matches, lost Kenneth Rosewall, quarter-final.

1975, did not play.

1976, seeded 10, won 2 matches, lost Bernie Mitton, 3rd round.

1977, did not play.

1978, seeded 16, won 3 matches, lost Raul Ramirez, 4th round.

Matches: 45–11; sets 148–54; games 1,230–935.

Longest Match: 1st round 1963, lost John Hillebrand 12–14 7–9 6–4 6–4 3–6 – a total of 71 games.

Age on first winning singles: 23 years 45 days.

Age on last winning singles: 27 years 41 days.

Overall Record:

	Titles	Matches		
		Played	Won	Lost
Singles	3	56	45	11
Doubles	6	66	52	14
Mixed	0	24	14	10
Total	9	146	111	35

Career Achievements:

The Championships, Wimbledon: singles 1967, 1970, 1971; doubles 1965, 1966, 1968–1970, 1974.

US Championships: singles 1967, 1973; doubles 1967, 1971, 1973; mixed 1964.

French Championships: doubles 1967, 1969, 1973.

Australian Championships: singles 1973, 1975; doubles 1965, 1967, 1971, 1973, 1976; mixed 1965.

Total Grand Slam titles: 26 – singles 7, doubles 17, mixed 2.

Italian Championships: singles 1969; doubles 1965, 1969, 1971, 1973; mixed 1964.

Australian Davis Cup team: 1963–1967, winning 25 from 34 matches (singles 16–7, 1 unf; doubles 9–2) in 15 ties.

Won: 32 singles titles, 41 doubles titles.

Played: 565 singles, winning 429 (Open Era).

Prize money: $1,062,408.

Full name: John David Newcombe

Born: 23rd May, 1944, Sydney, NSW, Australia.

Stan Smith

1972

Pillar of Strength

One would need to go far to find a player more staunch, more solidly courageous than the 6 feet 4 inch Stan Smith from Pasadena, where the big telescope is, in California. One could well argue that he brought off one of the finest sporting feats of the century in winning the Davis Cup for the United States in 1972.

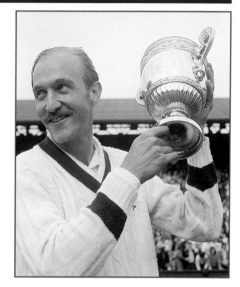

It was the first of the Finals as distinct from the Challenge Rounds and the US for political reasons, had given up their right to play at home. The team journeyed to Romania, to Bucharest, where, led by a brilliant but controversial Ilie Nastase and a ruthless Ion Tiriac, the home team were urged to victory by an outrageously partisan crowd. Further the linesmen were equally partisan and with armed guards around the court the efforts of the referee to restore a semblance of fair play were negatived by the intimidatory martial atmosphere.

Nonetheless Smith beat Nastase in the opening singles, won the doubles with Erik Van Dillen, in what was probably the most perfect performance of any doubles pair at any time, and took his second singles against Tiriac despite Romanian efforts to weaken him. The dreadful line decisions were only part of the difficulties he faced. Smith's success gave America the trophy and it was virtually a single handed effort by him. As a valiant sporting effort it can never have been matched in lawn tennis.

Smith pulled off that heroic success some three months or so after winning Wimbledon. He beat Nastase in the final and it was among the best ever seen. Smith had his luck. He looked likely to be trailing love-40 and falling to 2–4 in the fifth set when he salvaged a point with a frantic volley off the wood. He went on to become a highly regarded champion, esteemed not only for his admirably aggressive and heavy shots but for his impeccable sporting attitude.

Apart from being one of the best finals in history Smith's triumph was had on a Sunday for the first time. Rain had brought postponement. It was Smith's eighth challenge.

Only in his first year, 1965, when he went down to the Mexican, Rafael Osuna, did he lose to any but a past or future champion. He lost twice to Roy Emerson, twice to Rod Laver and twice to John Newcombe. He was in the final against the last just twelve months before his own success.

Smith did not defend in 1973 because loyalty to the Association of Tennis Professionals meant he had to take part in the boycott. No man was welcomed back more warmly in 1974 but at 27 and ten years from his debut the edge of his axe was blunted – far more so than that of the far older Ken Rosewall who beat him in a windswept semi-final.

Smith competed for the 19th time in 1983 but lost in the first round. The singles was his only Wimbledon title, surprisingly because he was a fine doubles exponent and four times a winner of his own American title. His partnership with his compatriot Bob Lutz was notable. In the course of 1968 they collected the US InterCollegiate title, the US Clay Court title and both the US National and open Championships.

His Davis Cup record is among the best, extending from 1968 to 1981. He played a total of 12 matches in the Challenge or Final Round when the issue was still live and was only thrice beaten.

Wimbledon Singles Record:

1965, unseeded, won 1 match, lost Rafael Osuna, 2nd round.

1966, unseeded, won 3 matches, lost Roy Emerson, 4th round.

1967, unseeded, won 2 matches, lost John Newcombe, 3rd round.

1968, unseeded, won 1 match, lost Rodney Laver, 2nd round.

1969, seeded 16, won 3 matches, lost Rodney Laver, 4th round.

1970, seeded 7, won 3 matches, lost Roy Emerson, 4th round.

1971, seeded 4, won 6 matches, lost John Newcombe, Final.

1972, seeded 1, won 7 matches, *champion* (sets 21–5; games 157–108).
1973, did not play.
1974, seeded 4, won 5 matches, lost Kenneth Rosewall, semi-final.
1975, seeded 7, won 0 matches, lost Byron Bertram, 1st round.
1976, seeded 16, won 3 matches, lost Jimmy Connors, 4th round.
1977, seeded 11, won 3 matches, lost Jimmy Connors, 4th round.
1978, unseeded, won 0 matches, lost GuillermoVilas, 1st round.
1979, unseeded, won 2 matches, lost Jose-Luis Clerc, 3rd round.
1980, seeded 15, won 2 matches, lost Brian Gottfried, 3rd round.
1981, unseeded, won 3 matches, lost John McEnroe, 4th round.
1982, unseeded, won 1 match, lost Hank Pfister, 2nd round.
1983, unseeded, won 0 matches, lost Trey Waltke, 1st round.

Matches: 45–17; sets 149–73; games 1,231–1004.

Longest Match: 1st round 1969, beat Allan Stone 20–22 6–4 9–7 4–6 6–3 – a total of 87 games.

Age on winning singles: 25 years 208 days.

Overall Record:

	Titles	Matches		
		Played	Won	Lost
Singles	1	62	45	17
Doubles	0	57	40	17
Mixed	0	5	3	2
Total	1	124	88	36

Career Achievements:
The Championships, Wimbledon: singles 1972.
US Championships: singles 1971; doubles 1968, 1974, 1978, 1980.
Australian Championships: doubles 1970.
Total Grand Slam titles: 7 – singles 2, doubles 5.
Year end Championships: singles 1970, doubles 1970.
US Davis Cup team: 1968–1973, 1975, 1977–1979, 1981, winning 35 from 42 matches (singles 15–4; doubles 20–3) in 24 ties.
Won: 39 singles titles, 61 doubles titles.
Played: 903 singles, winning 640 (Open Era).
Prize money: $1,774,881.

Full name: Stanley Roger Smith
Born: 14th December, 1946, Pasadena, California, USA.

Jan Kodes

1973

The Boycott Champion

In 1973 the newly formed Association of Tennis Professionals called on their members to boycott the Wimbledon Championships following the suspension of Nikki Pilic by the Yugoslav Federation for allegedly failing to appear for a Davis Cup tie. They did so as a matter of principle and not out of animosity to a well liked meeting; in retrospect the matter, which aroused high feelings at the time, can be seen as part of the readjustment of the game following the abolition of the amateur-professional distinction.

Be that as it may, 79 leading players withdrew their entry and the draw had to be postponed and the seeding changed beyond recognition. So far as the general standard of men's play was concerned it was a travesty of former values. That cannot be gainsaid, though for all that it was a meeting of high interest, strongly supported and productive of a winner whose name is not out of place amid its distinctive company.

Jan Kodes, a clay court specialist from Czechoslovakia, became the boycott champion. A winner *faute de mieux*? Hardly that, for he had twice been singles champion of France, in 1970 and 1971, and in the latter year had shown high flair by beating John Newcombe, the top seed, in the first round of the US Open on the grass at Forest Hills and going on to reach the final there against Stan Smith.

He had lost to the same man in the 1972 semi-final at Wimbledon. Kodes was among those clay court men who liked to say 'grass is only fit for cows' but who nonetheless did better than most players on it.

He showed no disloyalty to ATP in competing since he had not been allowed by the Czech authorities to become a member. His seeding position was number two, his highest ever, with Ilie Nastase at number one. The Romanian took that burden of expectation uneasily and went out in the fourth round to the American Sandy Mayer. Mayer in turn lost to the Russian Alex Metreveli, the fourth seed.

Kodes had no special peril until he met the third seed, Roger Taylor, in the semi-finals. The British No.1 had been a narrow fifth set quarter-final victor against Bjorn Borg. Kodes was threatened all the way by Taylor. He lost the first set after having two set points and was 4–5 behind in the fifth when rain stopped play.

His Warsaw Pact national final against Metreveli was neither a great match nor a bad one. Metreveli bore all the signs of being inhibited by the occasion. Kodes, the more experienced at that level of the game, played an able match and was rewarded with the crown. One can only assume that but for the boycott he would not have triumphed as he did. But he was in no way not worthy of the honour.

He acquired his crown when he was 27 and playing for the eighth time. His last singles was in 1981 when he was 35. At his home in Prague he constructed his own grass court. As with Santana before him what was good enough for cows was good enough for him.

He was a player of precise excellence, by no means a heavyweight but certainly not a lightweight. He was the first men's singles champion to be inscribed as 'Czechoslovakia' in the draw sheet, for his national predecessor in that role, Jaroslav Drobny, as a refugee, had to foreswear that tag when he was the winner in 1954.

Wimbledon Singles Record:

1966, unseeded, won 0 matches, lost Clifford Drysdale, 1st round.

1967, unseeded, won 0 matches, lost Anthony Roche, 1st round.

1968, unseeded, won 0 matches, lost Martin Riessen, 1st round.

1969, unseeded, won 1 match, lost Robert Lutz, 2nd round.

1970, seeded 13, won 0 matches, lost Alex Metreveli, 1st round.

1971, unseeded, won 0 matches, lost Thomas Okker, 1st round.

1972, seeded 5, won 5 matches, lost Stanley Smith, semi-final.

1973, seeded 2 won 7 matches, *champion* (sets 21–6; games 162–114).

1974, seeded 6, won 4 matches, lost Jimmy Connors, quarter-final.

1975, seeded 12, won 1 matches, lost Geoffrey Masters, 2nd round.

1976, did not play.

1977, unseeded, won 0 matches, lost Guillermo Vilas, 1st round.

1978, unseeded, won 0 matches, lost Jaime Fillol, 1st round.

1979, unseeded, won 0 matches, lost Hank Pfister, 1st round.

1980, unseeded, won 1 match, lost Victor Pecci, 2nd round.

1981, unseeded, won 0 matches, lost Vijay Amritraj, 1st round.

Matches: 19–14; sets 68–58; games 638–588.

Longest Match: Semi-final 1973, beat Roger Taylor 8–9 9–7 5–7 6–4 7–5 – a total of 67 games.

Age on winning singles: 27 years 128 days.

Overall Record:

	Titles	Matches Played	Won	Lost
Singles	1	33	19	14
Doubles	0	27	13	14
Mixed	0	10	7	3
Total	1	70	39	31

Career Achievements:

The Championships, Wimbledon: singles 1973.

French Championships: singles 1970, 1971.

Total Grand Slam titles: 3 – singles 3.

Czechoslovak Davis Cup team: 1966–1980, winning 60 from 94 matches (singles 39–19, 2 unf; doubles 21–15) in 39 ties.

Won: 9 singles titles, 17 doubles titles.

Played: 640 singles, winning 405 (Open Era).

Prize money: $673,197.

Full name: Jan Kodes
Born: 1st March 1946, Prague, Czechoslovakia.

Jimmy Connors

1974, 1982

Consistent Power

Between January 1972, when he won a tournament in Jacksonville, Florida, and September 1983, when he won the US Open title for the fifth time, Jimmy Connors had 100 tournament victories.

Double-fisted on a trenchant backhand, his uncompromising power hitting, which marked his play from the first, perhaps flourished most in his own country. It is noteworthy, though, that five singles wins in the

US Open were gained on three different surfaces, on grass in 1974, on 'Har-Tru' (an American version of clay) in 1976 and on cement at Flushing Meadows in 1978, 1982 and 1983. It is a record that still stands.

This left-hander, from Belleville, Illinois, a town not far from St. Louis, competed first in the US Open meeting in 1970 when he was just short of 18. He reached the quarter-finals in 1973. In the next ten years he was never less than a semi-finalist and won five out his seven finals.

His consistency was unparalleled at Wimbledon. After a false start in 1971 when as Intercollegiate US Champion he failed to show, he earned a quarter-final singles place at his debut the next year. In 1982 he won for the second time without ever falling before the quarter-finals and mostly doing a good deal better. His loss in the fourth round to Kevin Curren in 1983 was his worst performance to that time.

Connors won Wimbledon in 1974 with something of a hollow victory over the Australian Ken Rosewall. At 39 years old Rosewall had burnt himself out in winning his semi-final against Stan Smith. Connors had found his quarter-final against Jan Kodes, then the defending champion, vastly harder. He had been in even more dire peril in the second round against Phil Dent of Australia, battling through after trailing one set to two only by 10–8 in the fifth set.

The Championships had a story book finish that year. Chris Evert, who won the women's singles, was then affianced to Connors. In more forthright lawn tennis terms both the champions had double-fisted backhands and from that time that grip, for long held to be a handicap, was established as entirely orthodox.

Connors yielded his title in the last match of 1975, when his fellow American, Arthur Ashe, beat him authoritatively in four sets. Connors was forced to reveal his weakness, if one could call it that. His forehand had fragile aspects, especially against short, low balls, and it marred his confidence.

In 1976 Connors lost in the quarter-finals to the hard serving Roscoe Tanner and by his own standards this was failure. In all of the next three years Connors had no cause to feel he had done less than he should. With Bjorn Borg in the full tide of his invincibility he lost to the Swede in 1977, 1978 and 1979, the first two of those years in the final. He ran Borg hard in 1977, yielding only in a 6–4 fifth set.

In 1980 John McEnroe was too good for him. In 1981 it was Borg again and this time, in the semi-finals. Connors took his New York rival to five sets without avail. When in 1982 Connors thrived once more, beating McEnroe after losing the first and third sets of the final, his exploit recalled that of Big Bill Tilden many years before. There was a gap of nine years between Tilden's second singles title of 1921 and his next in 1930. Connors had crossed a gap of eight years and was 31 years old.

Connors inflicted his game on his opponents, never ceasing to project winners with heavyweight strokes or, if losing, going down with all guns firing. He took defeat grudgingly but never with malice.

Wimbledon Singles Record:

1971, withdrew.
1972, unseeded, won 4 matches, lost Ilie Nastase, quarter-final.
1973, seeded 5 won 4 matches, lost Aleksandr Metreveli, quarter-final.
1974, seeded 3, won 7 matches, *champion* (sets 21–7; games 164–107).
1975, seeded 1, won 6 matches, lost Arthur Ashe, final.
1976, seeded 2, won 4 matches, lost Roscoe Tanner, quarter-final.
1977, seeded 1, won 6 matches, lost Bjorn Borg, final.
1978, seeded 2, won 6 matches, lost Bjorn Borg, final.
1979, seeded 3, won 5 matches, lost Bjorn Borg, semi-final.
1980, seeded 3, won 5 matches, lost John McEnroe, semi-final.
1981, seeded 3, won 5 matches, lost Bjorn Borg, semi-final.

1982, seeded 2, won 7 matches, *champion* (sets 21–4; games 150–88).
1983, seeded 1, won 3 matches, lost Kevin Curren, 4th round.
1984, seeded 3, won 6 matches, lost John McEnroe, final.
1985, seeded 3, won 5 matches, lost Kevin Curren, semi-final.
1986, seeded 3, won 0 matches, lost Robert Seguso, 1st round.
1987, seeded 7, won 5 matches, lost Patrick Cash, semi-final.
1988, seeded 5, won 3 matches, lost Patrick Kuhnen, 4th round.
1989, seeded 10, won 1 match, lost Daniel Goldie, 2nd round.
1990, did not play.
1991, unseeded, won 2 matches, lost Derrick Rostagno, 3rd round.
1992, unseeded, won 0 matches, lost Luis-Enrique Herrera, 1st round.

Matches: 84–18; sets 265–94; games 2,011–1,435.

Longest Match: 4th round 1988, lost to Patrick Kuhnen 7–5 6–7 6–7 7–6 3–6 – a total of 60 games.

Age on first winning singles: 21 years 307 days.

Age on last winning singles: 29 years 305 days.

Overall Record:

	Titles	Matches		
		Played	Won	Lost
Singles	2	102	84	18
Doubles	1	16	12	4
Mixed	0	5	4	1
Total	3	123	100	23

Career Achievements:
The Championships, Wimbledon: singles 1974, 1982; doubles 1973.
US Championships: singles 1974, 1976, 1978, 1982, 1983; doubles 1975.
Australian Championships: singles 1974.
Total Grand Slam titles: 10 – singles 8, doubles 2.
Year end Championships: singles 1977.
US Davis Cup team: 1976, 1981, 1984, winning 10 from 13 matches (singles 10–3) in 7 ties.
Won: 109 singles titles, 19 doubles titles.
Played: 1491 singles, winning 1222.
Prize money: $8,641,040.

Full name: James Scott Connors
Born: 2nd September 1952, East St. Louis, Illinois, USA.

Arthur Ashe

1975

The Man Who Came Back

Arthur Ashe was a distinctive champion in more than one way. First he was black and the only one of his colour to win the men's singles. Not that much was made of that because the first black singles champion at Wimbledon was among the women in the 1950s, Althea Gibson. Nor did it loom large at Wimbledon in 1975. Ashe's race meant more when he was a youngster building his game at a time in the United States when to be coloured brought social difficulties.

His black status was brought to deliberate prominence when he was denied a visa to go to South Africa in 1970. In 1973 he was successful and he reached the final of the South African title meeting against Jimmy Connors.

Ashe's second distinction as a champion at Wimbledon was to win at the age of 31 when he seemed to have passed his peak. In 1968, when as a serving officer in the US Army he played as an amateur, he was a brilliant winner of the first US Open Championship at Forest Hills. In both that year and the following he went near the summit at Wimbledon, losing to Rod Laver in the semi-finals in both years. The 1969 contest was among the most spectacular. In a burst of unbelievably fast pace-making Ashe won the first set. Laver took the second with an even more dynamic display of hard hitting and the issue was virtually settled in an even confrontation of virtuosity in the third set, with Laver eventually winning 2–6 6–2 9–7 6–0.

Thereafter Ashe's success diminished and he appeared to be a declining force. In 1973 he was the leading activist, if one can use that term, in the boycott action of the Association of Tennis Professionals against Wimbledon. Not that anything like personal animosity was raised in that stormy issue.

His 1975 triumph was a *tour de force* in the last three rounds. In the quarter-finals he beat the third seeded Bjorn Borg (Ashe himself was the number six) who had just won the French title for the second year. His semi-final was a demanding struggle against the Australian left-hander Tony Roche, the score 6–4 in the fifth set. In the final Ashe met Connors, the thrusting champion of 1974 of not only

Wimbledon but the US Open as well. Ashe was nine years older and he played a superb tactical match.

He exploited to the full the vulnerable aspects of Connors' forehand and his liking for pace. Ashe enmeshed his man and was a brilliant winner in four sets.

Ashe last competed in the singles in 1979 at the age of 35, by which time he had come to be regarded as a Wimbledon institution. Subsequently he had to undergo heart surgery and the triple by-pass operation proved to be the cause of his untimely death. The blood transfusions were infected with the Aids virus and it was this that eventually killed him at the age of 49.

The proponents of black freedom have reason to look on Ashe as a man who did good service for their cause. In the Wimbledon context he was one of those fine Americans who combine their high skills with impeccable sportsmanship.

Wimbledon Singles Record:

1963, unseeded, won 2 matches, lost Charles McKinley, 3rd round.
1964, unseeded, won 3 matches, lost Roy Emerson, 4th round.
1965, unseeded, won 3 matches, lost Rafael Osuna, 4th round.
1966, 1967, did not play.
1968, seeded 13, won 5 matches, lost Rodney Laver, semi-final.
1969, seeded 5, won 5 matches, lost Rodney Laver, semi-final.
1970, seeded 3, won 3 matches, lost Andre Gimeno, 4th round.
1971, seeded 5, won 2 matches, lost Martin Riessen, 3rd round.
1972, 1973, did not play.
1974, seeded 8, won 2 matches, lost Roscoe Tanner, 3rd round.
1975, seeded 6, won 7 matches, *champion* (sets 21–6; games 159–108).
1976, seeded 1, won 3 matches, lost Vitas Gerulaitis, 4th round.
1977, did not play.
1978, seeded 15, won 0 matches, lost Steve Docherty, 1st round.
1979, seeded 7, won 0 matches, lost Chris Kachel, 1st round.

Matches: 35–11; sets 112–62; games 1,001–842.

Longest Match: 3rd round 1969 beat G.R. Stilwell 6–2 1–6 6–2 13–15 12–10 a total of 73 games.

Age on winning singles: 31 years 360 days.

Overall Record:

	Titles	Matches Played	Won	Lost
Singles	1	46	35	11
Doubles	0	29	18	11
Mixed	0	5	3	2
Total	1	80	56	24

Career Achievements:

The Championships, Wimbledon: singles 1975.
US Championships: singles 1968.
French Championships: doubles 1971.
Australian Championships: singles 1970; doubles 1977.
Total Grand Slam titles: 5 – singles 3, doubles 2.
US Davis Cup team: 1963, 1965–1970, 1975, 1977, 1978, winning 28 from 34 matches (singles 27–5; doubles 1–1) in 18 ties.
Won: 33 singles titles, 18 doubles titles.
Prize money: $1,584,956.

Full name: Arthur Robert Ashe
Born: 10th July, 1943, Richmond, Virginia, USA.
Died: 13th February, 1993, New York, New York, USA.

Bjorn Borg

The Master Champion

Never in the history of lawn tennis did any player accomplish so much and in so brief a time as the Swede Bjorn Borg. He was more coolly dominating and ruthless at Wimbledon than any modern challenger, precociously successful in clay court meetings like the Italian and French, clinically efficient in the Davis Cup and entirely a sporting phenomenon.

Unwittingly, probably, he took the earnings of professional players to unprecedented levels and had become a millionaire in his early twenties. With his rugged skill, based on top spin, fitness and unyielding determination, his example made the double fisted backhand and patience an orthodoxy.

He was only 15 when he first played for Sweden in the Davis Cup in 1972. His debut against New Zealand saw him win both his singles matches. Three years later his prowess was the main instrument by which Sweden won the trophy.

He was still short of his 17th birthday when he won the Italian title in Rome in 1974, only just 17 when he won the French Championships a few weeks later. He took the French title for the sixth time in 1981. His failures were concentrated into the US Open meeting. He competed there ten times, 1972 to 1981, and never won; he lost in the final in 1976, 1978, 1980 and 1981.

Borg, idolised by young spectators and awesomely admired by all, was never out of countenance, not even in defeat, a state of affairs he experienced but seldom. Wimbledon knew him mainly as a bearded Swede, for he was prone to eschew shaving for the duration of the meeting.

He was very young when he first took the feel of the Wimbledon courts. He was there in 1971 as a junior when only 15. He lost to the Brazilian J Basgabo-Fillol in the first round of the invitation junior tournament. A year later he showed his paces and won the final against Buster Mottram, hauling up from 2–5 in the third set.

He first played in The Championships in 1973, aged 17. That was the boycott year and because of that the precocious talents of Borg were rewarded with the number six seeding place. He justified the choice and his loss in the quarter-finals to the British No.1, Roger Taylor, was in a close 7–5 fifth set.

In 1974 Borg was an established champion, holder of both the Italian and French titles. The burden of expectation proved too much and as early as the third round he could hardly get off the court fast enough against the Egyptian, Ismail El Shafei. Again in 1975 there was just a hint that the weight of having much to lose bore heavily on him. On the seeding he should have beaten Arthur Ashe in the quarter-finals but the American beat him – and, indeed, went on to take the title.

Borg in 1976 wove the first strands in his unique Wimbledon tapestry. He began by beating David Lloyd 6–3 6–3 6–1 in the first round. He did not taste defeat until the final against John McEnroe in 1981, by which time he had won 41 matches in sequence and taken The Championship five times. The span between his defeats was from July 1st 1975 when Ashe beat him, to July 4th 1981 with McEnroe his victor. 41 matches in a continuity of success! The US Independence Day in 1981 was like an era coming to an end, an era of Borg the unconquerable.

His first triumph in 1976 was statistically his easiest. He lost a set to no-one, with Guillermo Vilas his victim in the quarters, the hard serving Roscoe Tanner in the semis and the touch genius Ilie Nastase in the final.

His subsequent championships were more onerously gained. In 1977 he lost the first two sets to the Australian Mark Edmondson in round two. Having again beaten Nastase in the quarters, he beat the American Vitas Gerulaitis in a five set semi-final – the score was 8–6 in the fifth – after a display of breathtaking brilliance by both men that made it a classic of perfection. In the final he survived a five setter against Connors.

In 1978 he made an awkward start and in the curtain-raiser of the meeting on the Centre Court trailed one set to two against Victor Amaya, a big American left-hander with a big service. He was more dominant thereafter and won the final again against Connors, this time quite easily.

The perturbations of his progress in 1979 were again early, in the second round where the Indian Vijay Amritaj led two sets to one. The final also had Borg against the ropes, Tanner building a two sets to one lead before Borg slew him.

In 1980 Borg had his notable confrontation with McEnroe in the final. It was among the best ever played at that stage. Borg, having recovered from a slow, bad start, was denied six match points in the fourth set.

The tension and excitement of the contest was transcendental. McEnroe won the set after a tie break extending to 18–16. (It was the second longest at

Wimbledon. The longest had been played by Borg himself as far back as 1973 when he took a tie break of 20–18 against the Indian Premjit Lall in the opening round.)

Borg won the final set by 8–6 to be champion for the fifth successive time, a record of unbroken success surpassing all other exploits.

There was the prospect until the last moment that Borg would further this awesome record to six in 1981. His sequence of invincibility was carried to 41 matches with a semi-final win over Connors. It was a close run affair, Borg rallying to win 0–6 4–6 6–3 6–0 6–4.

In the final against McEnroe's left-handed sharpness Borg closed his Wimbledon account, with the American winning 4–6 7–6 7–6 6–4. For

Wimbledon a Swedish world had come to an end. By the next meeting the game's most successful player had retired. He was only just 25 when he played his last Wimbledon.

There have been champions more stimulating in their style of play. None was so impeccably ruthless as Borg. He was a master champion.

Wimbledon Singles Record:
1973, seeded 3, won 4 matches, lost Roger Taylor, quarter-final.
1974, seeded 5, won 2 matches, lost Ismail El Shafei, 3rd round.
1975, seeded 3, won 4 matches, lost Arthur Ashe, quarter-final.
1976, seeded 4, won 7 matches, *champion* (sets 21–0; games 133–70).
1977, seeded 2, won 7 matches, *champion* (sets 21–6; games 162–115).
1978, seeded 1, won 7 matches, *champion* (sets 21–3; games 144–91).
1979, seeded 1, won 7 matches, *champion* (sets 21–6; games 152–102).
1980, seeded 1, won 7 matches, *champion* (sets 21–4; games 151–95).
1981, seeded 1, won 6 matches, lost John McEnroe, final.

Matches: 51–4; sets 152–42; games 1,149–801.

Longest Match: Final 1980, beat John McEnroe 1–6 7–5 6–3 6–7 8–6 – a total of 55 games.

Age on first winning singles: 20 years 27 days.

Age on last winning singles: 24 years 29 days.

Overall Record:

	Titles	Matches		
		Played	*Won*	*Lost*
Singles	5	55	51	4
Doubles	0	6	4	2
Mixed	0	5	3	2
Total	5	66	58	8

Career Achievement
The Championships, Wimbledon: singles 1976–1980.
French Championships: singles 1974, 1975, 1978–1981.
Total Grand Slam titles: 11 – singles 11.
Year end Championships: singles 1979, 1980.
Italian Championships: singles 1974, 1978.
Swedish Davis Cup team: 1972–1975, 1978–1980, winning 45 from 56 matches (singles 37–3; doubles 8–8) in 21 ties.
Won: 62 singles titles, 4 doubles titles.
Played: 700 singles, winning 576.
Prize money: $3,655,751.

Full name: Bjorn Rune Borg
Born: 6th June, 1956, Sodertalje, Sweden.

John McEnroe

1981, 1983, 1984

Temperamental Genius

No young player made so striking a debut at Wimbledon than did this sharp New Yorker in the centenary year of 1977. His superb left-handed skills had made themselves evident in the junior ranks and it was as a junior, aged 18, that the USTA sent him to Europe. He made his mark first in the French Championships in Paris when he took a Grand Slam title at his first bid, the mixed doubles. He won with his Douglaston, NY neighbour, Mary Carillo.

That, in the eyes of many, was not serious sporting business. He came to Wimbledon primarily to compete in the Junior Tournament. Many great players have dipped their toes into Wimbledon waters by that means, Rod Laver and Bjorn Borg, to name but two others.

McEnroe was destined to by-pass the juniors in a spectacular manner. He had also entered the qualifying competition and after winning his three rounds he thus came into The Championships proper. As he flourished all notions of the junior event went by the board.

His dash and flair and competitive edge took the tyro McEnroe through round after round, no less than five. For the first time in any major event a newcomer who was both a junior and a qualifier took himself into the heights of a semi-final. There he yielded to the weighty arts of Jimmy Connors and acquitted himself well enough to take the issue to four close sets.

When this remarkable young man came back a year later the eyes of the world were upon him. He lost in the first round. There were more grounds for real disappointment in 1979 when, now 20 years old and with a load of experience behind him, he had status as the number two seed but lost, rather tamely, to Tim Gullikson, the right-handed of the Wisconsin twins.

The fulfilment of his high talents was in 1980, even if climaxed in a loss. He reached the final that year and in a glorious contest he won a fourth set in a tie break 18–16 and lost 6–8 in the fifth set to Borg. It was one of the best matches in the game's history and winner and loser had equally to be honoured.

By the end of 1980 McEnroe had twice won his own US Open title at Flushing Meadows. Significantly in the 1980 final he beat Borg. Thus it was that in 1981 McEnroe won his first Wimbledon singles. He was never taken beyond four sets, not even in the final where Borg came to the end of half a decade's entire invincibility.

It was not, though, only in his image as a great lawn tennis player that McEnroe painted rich hues. Never in the history of the sport was there so public a display – taken round the world by television – of bad court manners when his temperament caused him to behave beyond acceptability in his opening match on Court One against Tom Gullikson. His offensiveness to the official – including the phrase 'You're the pits of the world' as a term of abuse – was established as an example of what sportsmanship should not be.

The outcome was an unprecedented step by the All England Lawn Tennis Club. Following his title success they did not, as was the custom, elect him an honorary member of the club.

In due course McEnroe, though never looking as if he would emulate Little Lord Fauntleroy, retrieved his standing. A year later the Club gave him the honour. By that time he had had another set back. He lost a stirring final to Jimmy Connors. Twelve months later he re-established himself as champion, this time losing one set in the course of it. By the end of 1983 McEnroe had two Wimbledon singles in his locker, had thrice taken the doubles with Peter Fleming and been a three times singles and doubles champion at Flushing Meadows. In addition he had thrice been the main instrument of the US triumph in the Davis Cup. His greatness was beyond dispute, especially on the doubles court. With Peter Fleming he won three Wimbledon, three US Open titles as well as seven consecutive Masters titles. Together in Davis Cup they lost only once in 15 outings, a remarkable achievement. Fleming once said modestly 'The greatest doubles pair in the world is John McEnroe and anyone'.

Michael Stich would certainly have agreed for in 1992 the German teamed with McEnroe at Wimbledon to win his only doubles title there. For McEnroe it was a fourth success and a glorious postscript to a glittering career.

His *annus mirabilis* was 1984. That year he won 13 of the 15 tournaments he contested and finished with a win/loss record of 82/3. Altogether he claimed 77 singles and 77 doubles titles, was ranked among the world's top ten for ten years and won altogether more than $12.5 million in prize money. With three Wimbledon singles (plus five doubles) and four US Opens (plus four doubles) as his record, his status among the all time greats is assured.

Wimbledon Singles Record:

1977, qualified, won 5 matches, lost Jimmy Connors semi-final.

1978, seeded 11 won 0 matches, lost Erik van Dillen, 1st round.

1979, seeded 2 won 3 matches, lost Tim Gullikson, 4th round.

1980, seeded 2, won 6 matches, lost Bjorn Borg, final.

1981, seeded 2, won 7 matches, *champion* (sets 21–3; games 148–97).

1982, seeded 1, won 6 matches, lost Jimmy Connors, final.
1983, seeded 2, won 7 matches, *champion* (sets 21–1; games 136–77).
1984, seeded 1, won 7 matches, *champion* (sets 21–1; games 134–63).
1985, seeded 1, won 4 matches, lost Kevin Curren, quarter-final.
1986, 1987, did not play.
1988, seeded 8, won 1 match, lost Wally Masur, 2nd round.
1989, seeded 5, won 5 matches, lost Stefan Edberg, semi-final.
1990, seeded 4, won 0 matches, lost Derrick Rostagno, 1st round.
1991, seeded 16, won 3 matches, lost Stefan Edberg, 4th round.
1992, unseeded, won 5 matches, lost Andre Agassi, semi-final.

Matches: 59–11; sets 184–56; games 1,390–966.

Longest Match: 2nd round 1980, beat Terry Rocavert 4–6 7–5 6–7 7–6 6–3 – a total of 57 games.

Age on first winning singles: 22 years 138 days.

Age on last winning singles: 25 years 143 days.

Overall Record:

	Titles	Matches Played	Won	Lost
Singles	3	70	59	11
Doubles	5	57	51	6
Mixed	0	9	7	2
Total	8	136	117	19

Career Achievements:

The Championships, Wimbledon: singles 1981, 1983, 1984; doubles 1979, 1981, 1983, 1984, 1992.
US Championships: singles 1979, 1980, 1981, 1984; doubles 1979, 1981, 1983, 1989.
French Championships: mixed 1977.
Total Grand Slam titles: 17 – singles 7, doubles 9, mixed 1.
Year end Championships: singles 1988, 1993, 1994, doubles 1978–1984.
US Davis Cup team: 1978–1984, 1987–1989, 1991, 1992, winning 59 from 69 matches (singles 41–8; doubles 18–2) in 30 ties.
Won: 77 singles titles, 77 doubles titles.
Played: 1059 singles, winning 867.
Prize money: $12,539,622.

Full name: John Patrick McEnroe
Born: 16th September 1959, Wiesbaden, West Germany.

Boris Becker

1985, 1986, 1989

The Young Master

On Sunday 7th July 1985 a German teenager made history by becoming the youngest man to win the Wimbledon singles title. Boris Becker was just 17 years 227 days old that sunny afternoon on Centre Court and his record is still intact. By beating South Africa's No. 8 seed Kevin Curren in four-sets Boris also became the first man from his country and the first non-seed to wear the most prestigious crown in tennis.

It had been another South African, Johan Kriek, who first recognized Becker's enormous potential. Following his loss to Boris in the Queen's Club final eight days before the start of the Championships (Becker's first tournament win on the men's Tour), the burly South African had said prophetically 'If Boris serves as well at Wimbledon as he did against me today he will win the title'.

How right he was! From Becker's first round win in four sets over the tall American Hank Pfister to his victory in the final against Curren, the tearaway teenager served like a demon. The headline writers had a field day. 'Boom Boom wins again' they blared as he bludgeoned his way past the American Matt Anger in straight sets and Sweden's No. 7 seed Joakim Nystrom 9–7 in the fifth to reach the fourth round. There he beat Tim Mayotte of the United States 6–2 in the fifth despite twisting an ankle and being two points from defeat in the fourth set tie-break. By now the crowds were warming to the youngster's infectious enthusiasm. They loved the Becker Boogie, that little dance of delight – fists clenched, feet pumping – after winning a particularly exciting rally. They oo'd and ah'd after every mighty ace – and there were many of those – and they roared their approval as he threw himself headlong diving for wide volleys.

Next it was a rain interrupted quarter-final win over Frenchman Henri Leconte in four sets and then semi-final success against the No. 8 seed from Sweden, Anders Jarryd, also in four sets, as a prelude to his ultimate triumph against Curren. By the time it was all over Boris had lost eight sets and 126 of the 292 games he had played, a losing game percentage of 43.15. Not even the 1949 winner Ted Schroeder, the only other champion to have lost as many as eight sets, had struggled so mightily. The American's losing percentage had been 40.89.

This was the start of what was to become a glorious career. By successfully defending his title the following year against world No.1 Ivan Lendl, Becker proved that he was a worthy champion. Five more Wimbledon finals in the next nine years were further proof of his worth on grass. The first three were all against his great Swedish rival, Stefan Edberg who beat him in 1988 and 1990, either side of Boris's third and last success in 1989. In 1991 Boris lost surprisingly to country-man Michael Stich in the first all-German final at Wimbledon and four years later he reached the final for the last time and lost in four sets to Pete Sampras, the man who had succeeded him as the king of Centre Court.

Born in Leimen, South Germany, only a couple of hours drive from Steffi Graf's birthplace of Neckarau, Boris learnt his tennis on the indoor court built near his home by his architect father, Karl-Heinz. It was there that his first coach Boris Breskvar encouraged him to dive for his volleys by placing gym mats at the side of the court on which to land. After winning the German junior championships three times, Gunther Bosch became his coach and Ion Tiriac started to manage his affairs. It was a management team that brought great success and great riches. At the height of his success a national poll revealed that Boris Becker was better known than the President of Germany. He was certainly richer. By the time he retired he had earned $25 million from prize money alone and many more millions from endorsements.

Becker's attacking game, built around his serve, good volleys, a powerful backhand and great athleticism brought him much success on fast surfaces, especially indoors. Three times in five years he led Germany to the final of the Davis Cup. Each time Sweden were the opponents. After a loss in Munich in 1985 Germany had revenge in 1988 in Gothenburg and won again the following year in Stuttgart.

Boris's three other Grand Slam wins came in 1989 at Flushing Meadows and in 1991 and 1996 in Melbourne, the first of those Australian successes with the help of coach Bob Brett who took Boris to the world No. 1 ranking that year. Although Boris reached the semi-finals of the French Open three times he could never find the consistency to win in Paris. In fact none of his 49 tournament wins from the 77 finals he contested were achieved on clay. It is the only gap in an otherwise impressive record.

Inevitably Boris was always in the news. During his seven year marriage to Barbara Feltus the problems they faced from racists in Germany were widely

publicised and caused them to leave the country for a time. His problems with the tax authorities were meat and drink to the German press as was Boris's whirlwind liaison with the Russian model, Angela Ermakova, at a restaurant in London. Nobu's broom cupboard had never before achieved such notoriety.

A spell as German Davis Cup captain and his work as a television personality has kept Boris in the public eye and his charitable work on behalf of youngsters in Germany helps him to retain his enormous popularity at home.

Wimbledon Singles Record:

1984, unseeded, won 2 matches, lost William Scanlon, 3rd round.
1985, unseeded, won 7 matches, *champion* (sets 21–8; games 166–126).
1986, seeded 4, won 7 matches, *champion* (sets 21–2; games 139–85).
1987, seeded 1, won 1 match, lost Peter Doohan, 2nd round.
1988, seeded 6, won 6 matches, lost Stefan Edberg, final.
1989, seeded 3, won 7 matches, *champion* (sets 21–2; games 141–88).
1990, seeded 2, won 6 matches, lost Stefan Edberg, final.
1991, seeded 2, won 6 matches, lost Michael Stich, final.
1992, seeded 4, won 4 matches, lost Andre Agassi, quarter-final.
1993, seeded 4, won 5 matches, lost Pete Sampras, semi-final.
1994, seeded 7, won 5 matches, lost Goran Ivanisevic, semi-final.
1995, seeded 3, won 6 matches, lost Pete Sampras, final.
1996, seeded 2, won 2 matches, lost Neville Godwin, 3rd round.
1997, seeded 8, won 4 matches, lost Pete Sampras, quarter-final
1999, unseeded, won 3 matches, lost Patrick Rafter, 4th round

Matches: 71–12; sets 222–74; games 1677–1255

Longest Match: 4th round 1994, beat Andrei Medvedev 6–7 7–5 7–6 6–7 7–5 – a total of 63 games.

Age on first winning singles: 17 years 227 days.

Age on last winning singles: 21 years 229 days.

Overall Record:

	Titles	Matches Played	Won	Lost
Singles	3	83	71	12
Doubles	0	2	1	1
Mixed	0	0	0	0
Total	3	85	72	13

Career Achievements:

The Championships, Wimbledon: singles 1985, 1986, 1989.
US Championships: singles 1989.
Australian Championships: singles 1991, 1996.
Total Grand Slam titles: 6 – singles 6.
Year end Championships: singles 1988, 1992, 1995.
German Davis Cup team: 1985–1989, 1991, 1992, 1995–1999, winning 54 from 66 matches, (singles 38–3; doubles 16–9) in 28 ties.
Won: 49 singles titles, 15 doubles titles.
Played: 927 singles, winning 713.
Prize money: $25,080,956.

Full name: Boris Franz Becker
Born: 22nd November, 1967, Leiman, West Germany.

Pat Cash

1987

Victorious Victorian

When he won the junior title at Wimbledon in 1982 it was clear that Pat Cash had a game tailor-made for grass. Strong and athletic, the Melbourne lad would race to the net behind a fast and accurate serve. Once there he would leap on his volleys like a tiger pouncing on its prey. His quick eye allowed him to see the ball early on his returns so his chip-and-charge tactics paid handsome dividends.

It was no surprise when, later the same year and still only 17, he won the men's grass court tournament in his home town to become the youngest winner of a Tour event. (It was a record that America's Aaron Krickstein would break the following year). The Kooyong crowd erupted. Here, surely, was a champion in the making. That impression was strengthened in 1983 when Pat beat Sweden's Joakim Nystrom in the fourth match of the Davis Cup final, again on the grass at Kooyong, to give Australia a winning 3–1 lead. Again the home town fans went wild with joy. Here, everyone thought, was the next John Newcombe. Once more Australia was set to rule the world.

When he reached the semi-finals at Wimbledon and the US Open in 1984 the Cash career seemed to be on course. At Wimbledon he had victories over Mats Wilander, Kevin Curren and Andres Gomez before John McEnroe outvolleyed him. At Flushing Meadows he beat Ilie Nastase, Brad Gilbert and Wilander again before losing to Ivan Lendl after holding a match point. The world No.1 saved it with an incredible lob at full stretch that he flicked over the head of the advancing Australian. Chasing back, Cash unleashed a forehand winner down the line . . . but it was just out!

There would be sweet revenge three years later at Wimbledon. Cash's Grand Slam triumph was the fulfilment of a childhood dream. It seemed to be written in the stars for the build-up had been perfect.

The previous December he had again been involved in Davis Cup drama. Once more Sweden were the opponents in Melbourne. Once more Cash would be the hero. After beating Stefan Edberg on the opening day Pat teamed with John Fitzgerald to beat Edberg and Anders Jarryd to give Australia a 2–1 lead. The following day he came back from two sets to one down to beat Michael Pernfors 6–3 in the fifth amid extraordinary scenes of jubilation among the spectators at Kooyong.

Even a loss in five sets to Edberg three weeks later in the Australian Open final could not dent Pat's confidence. His performances in Melbourne were all the more remarkable because three weeks before Wimbledon that year he had undergone an emergency appendectomy. Undismayed, he had competed there and reached the quarter-finals.

Accordingly, at Wimbledon 1987, now fully fit and bursting with Davis Cup pride, he feared no-one on a grass tennis court. Peaking at exactly the right moment he swept majestically through the last three rounds without dropping a set. His victims? Three world No. 1s – Wilander, Connors and Lendl. When Cash climbed over the heads of the spectators to embrace his coach Ian Barclay and his father in the players' guest box he set a precedent that others would follow.

At the time of his victory Cash was only the second Wimbledon junior champion after Bjorn Borg to win the men's singles. Since, both Stefan Edberg and Roger Federer have achieved the feat.

This proved to be the peak of Pat's career. A second loss in the final in Melbourne the following January was a bitter disappointment. At the end of a magnificent battle Wilander prevailed 8–6 in the final set. This was the first year on Rebound Ace at the new headquarters of Australian tennis in Flinders Park. One can only speculate about the likely outcome if the Championships had been still played on the grass at Kooyong. Although the Swede had twice won the title there in 1983 and '84, Cash held a 3–1 edge against him on grass.

Injuries and family problems would be the crosses that Pat would have to bear for the remainder of his career. Arthroscopic surgery on a knee and a torn Achilles tendon ruined his year in 1988. An elbow injury early in 1989, followed by a ruptured Achilles, kept him out for seven months at a time when he had separated from his long-time partner Anne Britt Kristiansen. He was not a happy man. Nor was happiness restored by his sixth and last tournament win in Hong Kong in 1990. He was ranked 243 at the time, the lowest ever to win a title. It was not the sort of record he was looking for.

Wimbledon Singles Record:
1983, unseeded, won 3 matches, lost Ivan Lendl, 4th round.
1984, unseeded, won 5 matches, lost John McEnroe, semi-final.
1985, seeded 6, won 1 match, lost Ricardo Acuna, 2nd round.

1986, unseeded, won 4 matches, lost Henri Leconte, quarter-final.

1987, seeded 11, won 7 matches, *champion* (sets 21–1; games 133–77).

1988, seeded 4, won 4 matches, lost Boris Becker, quarter-final.

1989, did not play.

1990, unseeded, won 3 matches, lost Boris Becker, 4th round.

1991, unseeded, won 1 match, lost Thierry Champion, 2nd round.

1992, unseeded, won 1 match, lost John McEnroe, 2nd round.

1993, 1994, did not play.

1995, unseeded, won 0 matches, lost Richard Norman, 1st round.

1996, did not play.

1997, unseeded, won 0 matches, lost Byron Black, 1st round.

Matches: 29–10; sets 95–41; games 766–577.

Longest Match: 2nd round 1991, lost to Thierry Champion 5–7 7–6 6–4 1–6 10–12 – a total of 64 games.

Age on winning singles: 22 years 39 days.

Overall Record:

	Titles	Matches Played	Won	Lost
Singles	1	39	29	10
Doubles	0	21	15	6
Mixed	0	3	2	1
Total	1	63	46	17

Career Achievements:

The Championships, Wimbledon: singles 1987.

Total Grand Slam titles: 1 – singles 1.

Australian Davis Cup team: 1983–1990, winning 31 from 41 matches (singles 23–7; doubles 8–3) in 19 ties.

Won: 7 singles titles, 11 doubles titles.

Played: 391 singles, winning 342.

Prize money: $1,949,370

Full name: Patrick Hart Cash

Born: 27th May, 1965, Melbourne, Victoria, Australia.

Stefan Edberg

1988, 1990

Elegance Personified

He was the quiet achiever and modest to a degree. When he won a tournament – and he collected 41 singles and 18 doubles titles during his distinguished career – Stefan Edberg looked almost embarrassed. It was a trait that endeared him to the fans who flocked in their thousands to watch him perform his serve-and-volley magic. In an age when modern racket technology was threatening to kill off the volleyer, Edberg's cultured game shone like a beacon of hope to volleyers everywhere. He proved that if you were good enough it could be done.

Edberg's career had begun promisingly. Sensibly heeding the advice of Percy Rosberg, the man who had first coached Bjorn Borg, Stefan changed from a double-handed backhand to a single-handed one. It would become one of the game's great strokes. After several domestic successes Stefan was launched internationally on the junior scene in 1983. He proceeded to capture all four major singles titles, the first boy to win a Junior Grand Slam since they had become Championship events in 1975. (America's Butch Buchholz had won all four in 1958 when they had been invitation tournaments).

Teaming up with former British Davis Cup player Tony Pickard as his coach, Edberg embarked upon a road of conquest that brought him six Grand Slam singles titles and three Davis Cup successes that stamped him as a world class performer. He and Mats Wilander carried between them the torch that Borg had first lit in Sweden ten years earlier.

Revelling in the fast conditions at Kooyong, Stefan won the last two Australian Championships played on grass at that historic arena. Curiously they were thirteen months apart, the first in December 1985 and the second in January 1987. There had been no Championship in 1986 to compensate for the fact that two had been held in 1977 when the Championship had moved to December. A return to the traditional January date was welcomed universally so that the Australian season could properly start the tennis year once again.

The first of those wins was against Wilander, who had held the title for the two previous years, the second was against the Australian No. 1 Pat Cash.

At Wimbledon Stefan's great rivalry with Boris Becker was the central theme of the late 1980s. Three times in a row they contested the final, the first time that this had happened since the abolition of the challenge round in 1922. Stefan won in 1988 and 1990, Becker in 1989 and all three were marvellous examples of attacking grass court tennis. The first of these meetings was played in two segments. After a rain delayed start on the Sunday it rained again and play was suspended with Becker leading 5–4. The atmosphere was flat on the Monday, a situation that seemed to affect Becker more than Edberg. Although the German won the first game to take that opening set he never looked comfortable against Edberg's persistent attack. The Swede duly won his first title comfortably in four sets.

In 1989 Stefan came to Wimbledon still smarting from a loss to 17-year-old Michael Chang in the French Open final two weeks earlier. Edberg had been seeded No. 3 and the firm favourite against the lowly 15th seed. But Chang was riding a wave of inspiration after putting out world No. 1 Ivan Lendl in the fourth round.

After beating Becker in the semis and then leading by two sets to one against Chang in the final, Edberg looked a certain winner. But the little American came back to win the last two sets 6–4 6–2 and, at 17 years 3 months, he became the youngest man to win a Grand Slam crown.

Perhaps it was that loss that left Edberg rather flat in the Wimbledon final as a majestic Becker crashed through his defences to inflict a 6–0 7–6 6–4 beating on the disconsolate Swede.

In 1990 Edberg was a different man. Playing the same confident attacking tennis that had brought him the title two years earlier, he won a full-blooded contest against his old foe 6–4 in the fifth set. The following month Stefan overtook Lendl atop the world rankings, a position he would occupy for 72 weeks altogether.

Edberg's finest hour came at the US Open in 1991. Having disposed of Lendl in a three set semi-final he destroyed Jim Courier in the final 6–2 6–4 6–0. The majestic Swede was letter-perfect as he swept through American defences. The out-and-out volleyer had beaten the master of the backcourt with something to spare. Another victory in New York the following year, this time in four sets against the young 1990 champion Pete Sampras was the last of Edberg's great Grand Slam performances. The lasting impression is that Stefan Edberg's name should have stood alongside Perry, Budge, Emerson, Laver and Agassi as the only men to have won all four Grand Slam titles. As Stefan himself admits, that unexpected loss to Chang in Paris in 1989 still rankles.

Stefan was a fine doubles player too, but like so many of the top ranked men, he stopped playing doubles in his later years because of the pressure to win singles titles. However, he did win the Australian and US Open doubles in 1987 with Anders Jarryd and in 1996 he teamed with Petr Korda to win a second Australian title in his farewell year.

Always a Davis Cup stalwart, Stefan appeared in seven finals, helping Sweden to victory on three occasions. In 1984 he partnered Jarryd in a key victory over Peter Fleming and John McEnroe, the only Davis Cup doubles loss suffered by that formidable American pair in 15 outings. Stefan also contributed to the 3–2 win over Germany in Munich in 1985 and to the 4–1 win over the Russians in Moscow nine years later. Altogether he played 35 ties in 13 years winning 35 of his 50 singles matches and 12 of his 20 doubles.

It is a mark of the respect in which he is held by his peers that the ATP Sportsmanship award that he won on several occasions has been named after him.

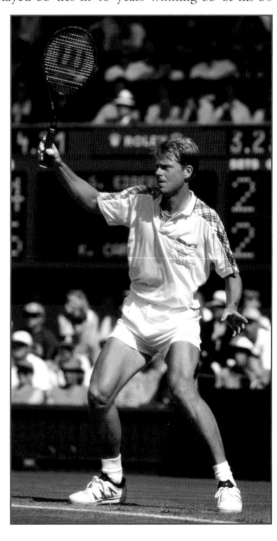

Wimbledon Singles Record:

1983, unseeded, won 1 match, lost Henrik Sundstrom, 2nd round.

1984, unseeded, won 1 match, lost Johan Kriek, 2nd round.

1985, seeded 14, won 3 matches, lost Kevin Curren, 4th round.

1986, seeded 5, won 2 matches, lost Miloslav Mecir, 3rd round.

1987, seeded 4, won 5 matches, lost Ivan Lendl, semi-final.

1988, seeded 3, won 7 matches, *champion* (sets 21–7; games 155–120).

1989, seeded 2, won 6 matches, lost Boris Becker, final.

1990, seeded 3, won 7 matches, *champion* (sets 21–5; games 148–89).

1991, seeded 1, won 5 matches, lost Michael Stich, semi-final.

1992, seeded 2, won 4 matches, lost Goran Ivanisevic, quarter-final.

1993, seeded 2, won 5 matches, lost James Courier, semi-final.
1994, seeded 3, won 1 match, lost Kenneth Carlsen, 2nd round.
1995, seeded 13, won 1 match, lost Richard Norman, 2nd round.
1996, seeded 12, won 1 match, lost Mikael Tillstrom, 2nd round.

Matches: 49–12; sets 159–60; games 1,236–920

Longest Match: 2nd round 1983, lost to Henrik Sundstrom 6–2 6–7 6–7 6–4 6–8 – a total of 58 games.

Age on first winning singles: 22 years 167 days.

Age on last winning singles: 24 years 170 days.

Overall Record:

	Titles	Matches		
		Played	Won	Lost
Singles	2	61	49	12
Doubles	0	13	8	5
Mixed	0	0	0	0
Total	2	74	57	17

Career Achievements:
The Championships, Wimbledon: singles 1988, 1990.
US Championships: singles 1991, 1992; doubles 1987.
Australian Championships: singles 1985, 1987; doubles 1987, 1996.
Total Grand Slam titles: 9 – singles 6, doubles 3.
Year end Championships: singles 1989, doubles 1985, 1986.
Olympic Games: singles 1988 bronze, doubles 1988 bronze.
Swedish Davis Cup team: 1984–1996, winning 47 from 70 matches, (singles 35–15; doubles 12–8) in 35 ties.
Won: 41 singles titles, 18 doubles titles.
Played: 1076 singles, winning 806.
Prize money: $20,630,941.

Full name: Stefan Bengt Edberg
Born: 19 January, 1966, Vasterik, Sweden.

Michael Stich

1991

Out of the Shadows

In tennis terms Michael Stich was a late developer. Despite winning the German junior championships in 1986 he decided to finish his education and complete his compulsory National Service before embarking on a sporting career.

One year younger than Boris Becker, Michael had grown up in the shadow of his precocious countryman. Accordingly he was a relatively unknown figure when, unseeded and unheralded, he won his first Tour title in Memphis in March, 1990.

One year later the whole of the tennis world had heard of Michael Stich. His remarkable straight sets victory at Wimbledon over three-time champion Becker in the first all-German final in the long history of The Championships was beamed to an incredulous TV audience around the world. It was a truly amazing performance, particularly when you remember that Stich had lost 6–1 6–2 to Becker in their only previous meeting on a fast indoor court the previous October in Paris.

From the start Michael was totally relaxed and totally focussed. As he stood at the net waiting for Becker to join him for the spin he smiled as his opponent searched anxiously in his bag for some missing article. He knew then that Becker was nervous. That was hardly surprising. Becker had everything to lose, Stich nothing.

Stich played impeccably that day. He out served Becker – quite a feat in itself – and his backhand returns and passes were devastating. A troubled Becker was never allowed to find any rhythm. The longer the match went on the more confused he became. The issue was never in doubt. In 151 minutes it was all over, a one-sided 6–4 7–6 6–4 victory full of blistering pace from the new champion. A stunned Becker could only shake his head and wonder what had gone wrong.

Three more tournament victories followed for Stich that year in Stuttgart, Schenectady and Vienna, successes that contributed to a year-end ranking of four, a career high at that stage. Although the following year he surrendered his

Wimbledon title at the quarter-final stage to a promising young American called Sampras, he teamed with John McEnroe to win the doubles in one of those unforgettable matches that will be spoken of in awe by those lucky ones who were there to witness it. With the score at 13–13 in the fifth set, their final against Americans Jim Grabb and Richey Reneberg, the No. 4 seeds, had been suspended at 9.21pm on the Sunday evening because of failing light. Already they had saved two match points on the Stich serve.

The match was completed on the third Monday. Entry to the No.1 Court stands was free and a capacity crowd of 6,500, composed largely of youngsters on a first visit to Wimbledon, all determined to enjoy themselves, created a wonderful atmosphere. Responding to their enthusiasm, the players produced some dazzling tennis. For 34 emotionally charged minutes the battle raged on. McEnroe was the General, nursing Stich through the tense moments with a jaunty but deadly serious intensity. With the crowd applauding every rally, like school kids at an end of term party, all four men produced moments of brilliance. The end came unexpectedly. McEnroe, going for a firm return, miss-hit the ball which became an unplayable lob. It left their unfortunate opponents stranded. Moments later it was all over. The unseeded pair had triumphed 5–7 7–6 3–6 7–6 19–17. It had been Wimbledon's longest ever doubles final both in terms of games (83) and duration (5h 1m). It was also a great piece of Wimbledon theatre.

One month later in Barcelona, Stich teamed with Becker to add an Olympic gold medal to his Wimbledon crown. Playing only their fourth tournament together the two singles champions combined well to beat the young South African pair Wayne Ferreira and Piet Norval in four sets. Even on the slow clay no pairs had found it easy to break a German serve.

There was also a golden end to 1992 for Stich. Victory in the Compaq Grand Slam Cup in Munich earned him a cool $2 million, the ideal way to start a marriage. It was easy to understand why Jessica, who had married Michael in September, was grinning from ear to ear as she applauded her husband's winners.

Perhaps inspired by those exploits Stich enjoyed an *Annus Mirabilis* in 1993. First he led Germany to the final of the World Team Cup in Dusseldorf, then went through the week undefeated in Frankfurt to win the ATP World Championship, beating Sampras in the final. Finally, back in Dusseldorf, he led Germany to victory in the Davis Cup final against Australia. By winning six of his eight finals that year on four different surfaces he ended the year as the world No. 2. At last he had escaped from Becker's shadow and was accepted at home as a true champion.

It proved to be the peak of Stich's career. Although he would appear in two more Grand Slam singles finals – at the US Open in 1994 where he fell to Andre Agassi and in Paris two years later where Russia's Yevgeny Kafelnikov beat him, the days of glory were over. After reaching the semi-finals at Wimbledon in 1997, injuries to his shoulder and an ankle forced him to retire.

Wimbledon Singles Record:

1989, unseeded, won 0 matches, lost Mikael Pernfors, 1st round.
1990, unseeded, won 2 matches, lost Guy Forget, 3rd round.
1991, seeded 6, won 7 matches, *champion* (sets 21–5; games 155–116).
1992, seeded 3, won 4 matches, lost Pete Sampras, quarter-final.
1993, seeded 6, won 4 matches, lost Boris Becker, quarter-final.
1994, seeded 2, won 0 matches, lost Bryan Shelton, 1st round.
1995, seeded 9, won 0 matches, lost Jacco Eltingh, 1st round.
1996, seeded 10, won 3 matches, lost Richard Krajicek, 4th round.
1997, unseeded, won 5 matches, lost Cedric Pioline, semi-final.

Matches: 25–8; sets 82–37; games 656–531.

Longest Match: Quarter-final 1993, lost to Boris Becker 5–7 7–6 7–6 2–6 4–6 – a total of 56 games.

Age on winning singles: 22 years 262 days.

Overall Record:

	Titles	Matches		
		Played	Won	Lost
Singles	1	33	25	8
Doubles	1	18	13	5
Mixed	0	0	0	0
Total	2	51	38	13

Career Achievements:

The Championships, Wimbledon: singles 1991; doubles 1992.
Total Grand Slam titles: 2 – singles 1, doubles 1.
Year end Championships: singles 1993.
German Davis Cup team: 1990–1996 winning 35 from 46 matches (singles 21–9; doubles 14–2) in 17 ties.
Won: 18 singles titles, 10 doubles titles.
Played: 561 singles, winning 385.
Prize money: $12,628,890.

Full name: Michael Detlef Stich
Born: 18th October 1968, Pinneberg, West Germany.

Andre Agassi

1992

Baseliner Supreme

Launched on an unsuspecting world in 1987 when he was still 16, a tearaway teenager complete with white baseball cap and blond pony tail, Andre Agassi would become the most charismatic player of his generation – indeed of any generation. By the time he was 35, and still competing at the highest level (he had reached his sixth US Open final in September 2005), Andre was already a legend.

With eight Grand Slam titles to his name, four in Melbourne, two at Flushing Meadows and one each at Roland Garros and Wimbledon, plus 17 Masters Series wins and one Tour Championship, Agassi had established his credentials as a true champion. Yet at the start there had been doubts.

Andre had been coached at first by his father Mike Agassian who had boxed for Iran in the 1948 and 1952 Olympics (the name was changed when the family emigrated to the United States). On the way to school each morning in Las Vegas Andre and his three older siblings Phillip, Rita and Tami, would go through their drills on court under the fierce gaze of their father. Woe betide anyone who didn't put everything into those sessions. Mike believed in developing the work ethic early.

When he was 13 Andre was sent to work with Nick Bollettieri, the flamboyant Florida coach whose training establishment was based at Bradenton. It was the perfect atmosphere for Andre to hone his skills for the work rate among Bollettieri's talented pupils was legendary.

That first year on the Tour revealed Agassi's skill as a match player. After reaching the final in Seoul on the eve of his seventeenth birthday, he produced some sparkling tennis four months later in Stratton Mountain to beat the newly crowned Wimbledon champion Pat Cash in two tie-break sets on his way to the semi-finals. There he took the middle set from World No.1 Ivan Lendl who was mightily relieved to win the decider 6–3. The kid who looked and acted like a young rock star had rocked the Establishment on its heels.

The first tournament success – on the hard courts of Itaparica in Brazil – came just six weeks later. In the next twelve months Agassi won six more titles, three of them on clay. Already Bollettieri's extravagant claims about Andre's potential seemed less preposterous.

Yet the loss to an ageing Andres Gomez in the French Open final of 1990 raised doubts about Agassi's self belief. Three months later a further damaging loss strengthened those doubts. This time it was a straight sets thrashing in the US Open final from junior rival Pete Sampras who, at 19, was one year younger than Andre. Bollettieri's grin had turned to a frown.

When the following year Agassi lost a second French Open final to Jim Courier, another junior rival who had trained with him and with Michael Chang at the Bollettieri Academy, the critics wrote him off as a spectacular failure. Bollettieri was in mourning.

Imagine, then, the sensation Andre caused when he walked away with the Wimbledon title in 1992. After losing in the first round to Henri Leconte in 1987, he had not played at Wimbledon for three years. Perhaps he had believed that his game of back court dominance would not work on grass. Returning in 1991 he had lost in the quarter-finals to David Wheaton. This had merely strengthened the doubts about his ability to win on the biggest occasions. Although treated on court for a thigh injury early in the first set Andre had served for the match at 6–5 in the fourth. After holding a 30–15 lead self belief died and he slumped to defeat 6–2 in the decider.

There were no such doubts in 1992. Serving powerfully and timing his returns and passes to perfection Andre was at last enjoying himself on grass. His tennis improved with each round and in his last three matches against two former champions, Boris Becker and John McEnroe, and the powerful Yugoslav left-hander Goran Ivanisevic, his timing and precision were extraordinary. There was a look of total disbelief on the faces of all three as, time after time, their best serves and approaches were rifled back past their groping rackets. At last Nick Bollettieri could afford to smile again.

Despite wrist surgery in December 1993 Andre was back to his best the following year. He had ended his association with Bollettieri somewhat acrimoniously and taken on board the shrewd former Tour player Brad Gilbert as his coach. Immediately they hit the jackpot. Among his five titles in 1994 was a first US Open crown. His straight sets win over Michael Stich was one of the most important in his career. Apart from being the first unseeded winner of the US title since 1966 when Fred Stolle had beaten fellow Australian John Newcombe, also unseeded, his victory established him in the minds of his countrymen as a champion.

A first visit to Australia in 1995 was crowned with success. In one of several transmogrifications that Andre underwent during his career he was now in his

pirate period. With bandana and colourful shirt and shorts, he lacked only a parrot on his shoulder and a cutlass between his teeth to complete the illusion. So imperious was his tennis that defending champion Sampras was made to walk the plank after being foolish enough to win the first set. Two months later Agassi assumed the No.1 ranking, a position he would occupy for 101 weeks all told.

A disastrous marriage in 1997 to movie starlet Brooke Shields, a grand-daughter of Frank Shields, plus further injury to his wrist contributed to Agassi's worst-ever year. His ranking slipped to 141 and he was reduced to playing Challenger events in an effort to restore his ranking.

In April 1999 he filed for divorce. The relief was reflected in his tennis. In June that year Andre came back from the loss of the first two sets against Andrei Medvedev in the final of the French Open to win the one major title missing from his portfolio. Ironically it was the one that everyone thought would be his first Grand Slam success eight years earlier. Thus he joined Perry, Budge, Laver and Emerson as the only men to have won all four of the major titles. Although he lost to Sampras in the Wimbledon final four weeks later the quality of his play that day established that he was once again a major force in the game.

So it has been ever since. By winning a second US Open title at the end of the year against his good friend Todd Martin, Agassi confirmed his growing assurance on the big occasions. There would follow three successes in Australia during the next four years and two more appearances in a US Open final as well as two appearances in winning US Davis Cup teams. His 46 hard court tournament wins among his total of 60 is an open era record. His 17 Masters Series successes provide another record. His nearest challenger was Sampras with just eleven.

The Agassi legend had grown to the point where he had become the father figure of the Tour. Since 2002 he has been coached by Darren Cahill who had ended his association with Lleyton Hewitt after taking the Australian to the top of the game. Agassi always credits Cahill for helping him to maintain his enthusiasm and self belief in his later years.

The other person he credits is his wife. His second marriage to Steffi Graf in October 2001 and the arrival of their two children Jaden Gill one week after the marriage (named after his dedicated trainer Gill Reyes, a one-time strength coach at the University of Las Vegas) and Jaz Elle in October 2003 gave Andre a new balance and a new perspective on life. He began to devote more time to the Foundation he had created in 1994 to assist underprivileged youngsters in Las Vegas. By the end of 2005 his friends in the music industry, who included Elton John, Celine Dion, Lionel Richie and Robbie Williams, had appeared at annual fund raising concerts and helped him to raise a massive $52.3 million for the project that now includes a High School jointly funded by the Nevada State government.

Wimbledon Singles Record:

1987, unseeded, won 0 matches, lost Henri Leconte, 1st round.
1988–1990, did not play.
1991, seeded 5, won 4 matches, lost David Wheaton, quarter-final.
1992, seeded 12, won 7 matches, *champion* (sets 21–6; games 156–111).
1993, seeded 8, won 4 matches, lost Pete Sampras, quarter-final.
1994, seeded 12, won 3 matches, lost Todd Martin, 4th round.
1995, seeded 1, won 5 matches, lost Boris Becker, semi-final.
1996, seeded 3, won 0 matches, lost Douglas Flach, 1st round.
1998, seeded 13, won 1 match, lost Tommy Haas, 2nd round.

1999, seeded 4, won 6 matches, lost Pete Sampras, final.
2000, seeded 2, won 5 matches, lost Pat Rafter, semi-final.
2001, seeded 2, won 5 matches, lost Pat Rafter, semi-final.
2002, seeded 3, won 1 match, lost Paradorn Srichaphan, 2nd round.
2003, seeded 2, won 3 matches, lost Mark Philippoussis, 4th round.

Matches: 44–12; sets 147–60; games 1147–867

Longest Match: 2nd round 2000, beat Todd Martin 6–4 2–6 7–6 2–6 10–8 – a total of 57 games.

Age on winning singles: 22 years 67 days.

Overall Record:

	Titles	Matches Played	Won	Lost
Singles	1	56	44	12
Doubles	0	0	0	0
Mixed	0	0	0	0
Total	1	56	44	12

Career Achievements:
The Championships, Wimbledon: singles 1992.
US Championships: singles 1994, 1999.
French Championships: singles 1999.
Australian Championships: singles 1995, 2000, 2001, 2003.
Total Grand Slam titles: 8 – singles 8.
Year end Championships: singles 1990.
Italian Championships: singles 2002.
Olympic Games: singles 1996, gold.
US Davis Cup team: 1988–1993, 1995, 1997, 1998, 2000, 2005 winning 30 from 36 matches (singles 30–6) in 22 ties.
Won: 60 singles titles, 11 doubles titles.
Played: 1126 singles matches, winning 860.
Prize money: $30,996,275.

Full name: Andre Kirk Agassi
Born: 29 April 1970, Las Vegas, Nevada, USA.

Pete Sampras

1993, 1994, 1995, 1997, 1998, 1999, 2000

The Aceman Cometh

For six glorious years Pete Sampras ruled the world of men's tennis. From 1993 to 1998 he ended the year atop the world rankings, a record that may never be equalled. He was, quite simply, a champion among champions.

At Wimbledon Sampras's record is unique. Seven times in eight years he made himself champion. He won 64 of the 71 matches he contested in 14 challenges. Although William Renshaw also won seven titles in nine years during the 1880s, the achievement of the champion from Cheltenham cannot be compared to that of Sampras. Renshaw was playing in the days of the Challenge Round so that five of his wins required only one match. His record was: played twenty-five matches, won twenty-two, lost three.

Sampras was born in Washington DC on 12th August 1971 of Greek parents who had emigrated to the United States. His father Sam and mother Georgia were nervous spectators. Accordingly they were present for only two of his eighteen Grand Slam finals. The first was his US Open loss to Stefan Edberg in 1992, the second his dramatic last Wimbledon win in 2000 against Australia's Pat Rafter when Pete was carrying an injury to his left shin. This 13th Grand Slam success ended in near darkness and took Pete past Roy Emerson's record of 12 major titles to secure his place in tennis history. To see the joy and relief on the faces of his parents as a tearful Pete scrambled up between the courtside spectators to embrace them in the stands was to know just how much they had suffered and how much it had meant to them all.

By the time of his 14th and last Grand Slam triumph in the US Open final of 2002 against Andre Agassi, Sampras was regarded by many as the greatest player the game had ever seen – certainly the greatest grass court player of all time. This had been his 64th tournament win and his fifth success at Flushing Meadows. He had also won two titles in Australia in 1994 and 1997 and five year-end Championships (only Lendl had won as many), and had helped the United States to two Davis Cup successes. The only trophy missing from his collection of silverware was a French Open Cup. The closest he got to success in 13 appearances at Roland Garros was a semi-final in 1996 when Russia's Yevgeny Kafelnikov proved too solid from the back of the court. Pete's attacking style was not suited to the slow clay in Paris and the very best baseliners could exploit a slight weakness on the backhand. On fast courts, however, he was supreme. The Sampras serve was acknowledged to have been the world's best. In 1993 he served a career-high 1,011 aces and two years later headed the list again with 974. The media christened him 'Pistol Pete'. But it was the second delivery that was so exceptional. Time after time in important matches, he would save break points with piercing deliveries that clipped the lines. He was utterly fearless. His other strengths included a fine volley, a wonderful running forehand, great athleticism, deceptive speed about the court and an indomitable will to win. As a serve-and-volley specialist he had no equal.

Yet as a youngster Sampras had played defensively from the baseline. In those days, like most of his contemporaries, he used a double-handed backhand. He freely admitted that Michael Chang, Jim Courier and the other leading juniors at the time were ahead of him. They could out-rally him.

In 1978, when Pete was six, Sam moved his family to Palos Verdes in California. They all joined the Peninsular Racquet Club where Pete developed his natural talents against his older brother and sister, Gus and Stella. When he was a young teenager competing in local junior tournaments he was spotted by Dr Pete Fisher, a family friend, who would become Sampras's first coach and mentor. Like Percy Rosberg with the young Edberg, Fisher realised that Pete had great potential as a volleyer and persuaded him to adopt a one-handed backhand. Fisher also encouraged him to watch tapes of the great Australian champion Rod Laver whose attacking game he hoped Pete could emulate. Laver became Pete's hero.

The improvement was rapid. Now that he was playing to his strengths Sampras was becoming a threat. A first semi-final appearance on the Tour at Schenectady in 1988, the year he turned professional as a 17-year-old, was followed by the capture of the Italian Open doubles title in Rome the following year with Courier.

Clearly Pete was growing in confidence. However, no-one was ready for what was about to happen in 1990. At Wimbledon that year he had lost in the first round for the second time. In his first appearance the previous year he had fallen to Australia's Todd Woodbridge. This time it was fellow American Richey Reneberg who beat him. At this stage Sampras had not discovered how to return serve on grass. It would take some patient work with coach Tim Gullikson, who started working with him in 1992, to solve that mystery.

Two months later at Flushing Meadows Sampras suddenly started to believe in himself. He powered his way to the quarter-finals for the loss of just one set to Thomas Muster. There he shocked three-time winner Ivan Lendl in a five set vic-

tory that ended Lendl's run of consecutive appearances in the US Open final at eight. Next he destroyed four-time champion John McEnroe in a four-set semi-final. Improbably the No.12 seed had arrived in the final to face one of his rivals from junior days. Andre Agassi may have been one year older but Sampras was the wiser. Continuing to set a blistering pace (he delivered 102 aces altogether during the tournament), Pete swept to the title in straight sets to achieve a childhood dream. At the age of 19 years and 28 days he had become the youngest man ever to win his national title.

His great rivalry with Agassi became a central theme of the men's game in the '90s. They met 34 times altogether with Sampras successful on 20 occasions, five of those wins coming in Grand Slam finals. Agassi's lone success in a title round had been on his first trip to Australia in 1995.

During the course of a spectacular career Sampras gave us some unforgettable moments. There was the time he cried on court early in the fifth set of his quarter-final against Jim Courier in Melbourne. 'Do it for your coach, Pete' someone had shouted, referring to Tim Gullikson who had just been diagnosed with a brain tumour and had been forced to fly home from Melbourne. Before he died the following year Tim told Pete that he was glad he had indeed done it for him that day in Melbourne. Thereafter Pete was coached by Paul Annacone

There was more drama in a night match at the US Open against Alex Corretja in 1966. Twice Pete had vomited on court. By the end of a gruelling battle that he won in a final set tie-break after saving a match point, Pete was absolutely exhausted. Afterwards he required half a gallon of intravenous fluids. It was then that everyone realised the strain he had always been under, as someone who suffered from Thalassemia Minor, an inherited blood disorder, similar to anaemia, that reduces the capacity of the body's red blood cells to carry oxygen.

Sampras himself believed that his best performance was his 6–3 6–4 7–5 title win at Wimbledon in 1999 against Agassi, played appropriately on 4th July. This was the match that brought him level with Emerson's twelve Grand Slams. 'Andre always brings out the best in me. He elevates my game to a level that is phenomenal. I could not have played any better' said the champion. All those who witnessed it would have agreed.

Sampras's place in the Pantheon of tennis champions is difficult to assess. His 14 Grand Slams and seven Wimbledon titles are both records. He shares another with the great Australian, Ken Rosewall. They are the only men who have won Grand Slam titles as teenagers, in their twenties and in their thirties. His prize money of $43,280,489 is yet another record. However, in assessing the greatest player of all time the lack of a French title must count against him. There are five men who have won all four of the major crowns, namely Fred Perry, Donald Budge, Rod Laver, Roy Emerson and Andre Agassi. Budge won the first Grand Slam in 1938 and Rod Laver achieved the feat twice – in 1962 as an amateur and in 1969 during

the second year of open tennis. In the end the decision has to be a matter of how you assess greatness.

Pete's greatness lay as much in the way he conducted himself at all times as in his record. Because he preferred to allow his racket to do the talking and avoided histrionics he was unfairly criticised for being dull.

Happily Pete was able to ignore the criticism and simply got on with his career and his life. In September 2000 he married Bridgitte Wilson, an actress. Their first child, Christian Charles, was born two years later. A second son, Ryan Nicholas arrived in 2005.

Wimbledon Singles Record:
1989, unseeded, won 0 matches, lost Todd Woodbridge, 1st round.
1990, seeded 12, won 0 matches, lost Christo van Rensburg, 1st round.
1991, seeded 8, won 1 match, lost Derrick Rostagno, 2nd round.

1992, seeded 5, won 5 matches, lost Goran Ivanisevic, semi-final.
1993, seeded 1, won 7 matches, *champion* (sets 21–4; games 147–103).
1994, seeded 1, won 7 matches, *champion* (sets 21–1; games 134–78).
1995, seeded 2, won 7 matches, *champion* (sets 21–6; games 160–109).
1996, seeded 1, won 4 matches, lost Richard Krajicek, quarter-final.
1997, seeded 1, won 7 matches, *champion* (sets 21–3; games 148–88).
1998, seeded 1, won 7 matches, *champion* (sets 21–3; games 145–104).
1999, seeded 1, won 7 matches, *champion* (sets 19–2; games 119–77).
2000, seeded 1, won 7 matches, *champion* (sets 21–4; games 147–103).
2001, seeded 1, won 3 matches, lost Roger Federer, 4th round.
2002, seeded 1, won 1 match, lost George Bastl, 2nd round.

Matches: 63–7; sets 194–49; games 1426–1009.

Longest Match: 4th Round 2001, lost Roger Federer 6–7 7–5 4–6 7–6 5–7 – a total of 60 games.

Age on first winning singles: 21 years 326 days.

Age on last winning singles: 28 years 332 days.

Overall Record:

	Titles	Matches		
		Played	Won	Lost
Singles	7	70	63	7
Doubles	0	3	2	1
Mixed	0	0	0	0
Total	7	73	65	8

Career Achievements:
The Championships, Wimbledon: singles 1993–1995, 1997–2000.
US Championships: singles 1990, 1993, 1995, 1996, 2002.
Australian Championships: singles 1994,1997.
Total Grand Slam titles: 14 singles -14.
Year end Championships: singles 1991, 1994, 1996, 1997, 1999.
Italian Championships: singles 1994, doubles 1989.
US Davis Cup team: 1991, 1992, 1994, 1995, 1997, 1999, 2000, 2002 winning 19 from 28 matches (singles 15–8; doubles 4–1) in 16 ties.
Won: 64 singles titles, 2 doubles titles.
Played: 984 singles, winning 762.
Prize money: $43,280,489.

Full name: Pete Sampras
Born: 12th August, 1971, Washington, DC, USA.

Richard Krajicek

1996

A Rare Dutch Master

He took us all by surprise. When Richard Krajicek arrived at Wimbledon in 1996 he was simply hoping to avoid embarrassment. The previous two years the tall Dutchman had lost in the opening round. Astonishingly, at the end of two action packed weeks he had made himself the champion, the first man from his country to capture a Grand Slam singles title.

There had been nothing to suggest such an improbable outcome. For a start, despite his world ranking of 13, Krajicek did not find his name among the list of 16 seeds. Originally he was in the draw at position No.12, with Britain's Chris Wilkinson as his first opponent. However, when Thomas Muster, the seventh seed, withdrew injured on the eve of the tournament, Richard, as the next highest ranked player of the non-seeds, was moved into Muster's position at No.32; lucky loser Anders Jarryd of Sweden became Wilkinson's opponent.

The new situation posed an interesting question. As the occupier of a seeded spot in the draw, was Krajicek himself now a seed? Before the tournament began a press release was issued by the Referee, Alan Mills, pointing out that the Grand Slam rule book made no provision for this eventuality. Accordingly, he said, Wimbledon had followed the practice of the ATP Tour where the player replacing a seed who had withdrawn did not himself become a seed. Paradoxically if this situation had arisen in the Ladies' Singles there would have been no ambiguity. On the women's Tour a seed who withdraws is replaced by the next highest ranked player and becomes the 17th seed.

As the Dutchman started upon his epic voyage of conquest that memorable year, the media regarded him as unseeded. During the second week, however, the Management Committee of The Championships issued another statement saying that Krajicek was, after all, a seed because he had occupied the position in the draw of a seeded player. In effect they were introducing a new rule to fill the void in the Grand Slam regulations.

This might have ended the confusion had the logical extension of that announcement been implemented. However, as Alan Little, the All England Club's Honorary Librarian pointed out several times, in the tournament programme Krajicek's name had not been emboldened to match the names of the other seeded players on the page. Nor was there a number alongside his name. Therefore, to the world at large, the Dutchman was still unseeded.

That is how it was reported in all the news media as Krajicek continued his amazing run past the 1991 winner Michael Stich in the fourth round, the reigning three-time champion Pete Sampras in the quarter-finals, Australia's unseeded interloper Jason Stoltenberg in the semis and then America's MaliVai Washington, also a non-seed, in the final. Inevitably the world's tennis writers, TV commentators and Radio broadcasters described it as the first Wimbledon final in history between two unseeded players. The fact that Wimbledon's post-Championships programme, complete with all the results, DID have Krajicek's name in bold type seemed to be a case of trying to re-write history.

There was another Wimbledon 'first' associated with the 1996 final. As Krajicek and Washington were posing at the net for the courtside photographers prior to the commencement of the match, a streaker dashed onto court, waving to the two astonished players as she ran towards the Royal Box and into the arms of the policeman guarding the players' entrance. Melissa Johnson may unwittingly have aided Krajicek in his quest. 'Actually I was very nervous. It was a Wimbledon final and as the favourite I had everything to lose. It kind of broke the tension' he said afterwards.

Everyone was full of praise for Krajicek's uncomplicated power game. He turned serve-and-volley tennis into an art form. The really astonishing thing about his win is that in those last four matches he did not drop a single set. In fact he lost only one set during the entire tournament – that to the New Zealander Brett Steven in the third round. Otherwise his blistering serves, powerful volleys and uncompromising returns and passes destroyed everything in their path. Rarely has a player lifted his game to such heights and maintained that standard for so long.

Especially impressive had been his win over Sampras. The champion simply could not read the direction of the Dutchman's serve and was dismayed to find some of his own best deliveries rifled back past him before he had ended his service swing. Krajicek's tactics had been delightfully simple. 'I knew that if you kept coming at his backhand then it would break down. That was basically my strategy' he said. It was a strategy that brought Krajicek six victories against Sampras in their ten career meetings to make him the only contemporary to hold a winning margin against the American.

The son of Czech immigrants, Richard had been born in Rotterdam and introduced to tennis at the age of four by an ambitious father who pushed him hard as a youngster. The capture of national under-12 and under-14 age group titles in

Holland suggested a bright future but a series of injuries would seriously impede his progress just as he seemed to be making a breakthrough.

At the Australian Championships in 1992 after beating Michael Stich in five long sets he was forced to pull out of his semi-final against Jim Courier with a damaged shoulder. There followed problems with both knees that required surgery in 1996, 1998 and 2000. These continual interruptions to his career were equally damaging psychologically. Elbow surgery in March 2001 kept him away from competition for 20 months and two months after his return in July 2002 a heel injury sustained at the US Open virtually ended his career.

Despite these problems Richard did reach a semi-final in Paris in 1993 and gave us one more memorable match at Wimbledon, a semi-final against Goran Ivanisevic in 1998. Coming back from the loss of the first two sets, Richard saved two match points in the third when Goran served at 5–3, 40–15 and then led with a break at 3–2 in the fifth before losing the decider 15–13. His Wimbledon win in 1996 proved to be the peak of Krajicek's career which brought him 17 singles titles altogether and three in doubles. He reached a career-high ranking of No.4 in 1999.

Also in 1999 Richard married the model, TV presenter and actress Daphne Deckers who appeared in the James Bond film 'Tomorrow Never Dies'. They have a daughter Emma and a son Alec. As well as being Tournament Director of the Tour event in Rotterdam, nowadays Krajicek devotes much of his spare time to the Foundation which bears his name and was launched in 1993 with the aim of helping disadvantaged Dutch youngsters who are keen on sport. This work earned him ATP's Arthur Ashe Humanitarian Award in 2000.

Wimbledon Singles Record:
1991, unseeded, won 2 matches, lost Andre Agassi, 3rd round.
1992, seeded 11, won 2 matches, lost Arnaud Boetsch, 3rd round.
1993, seeded 9, won 3 matches, lost Andre Agassi , 4th round.
1994, unseeded, won 0 matches, lost Darren Cahill, 1st round.
1995, seeded 12, won 0 matches, lost Bryan Shelton, 1st round.
1996, seeded 4, won 7 matches, *champion* (sets 21–1; games 137–87).
1997, seeded 4, won 3 matches, lost to Tim Henman, 4th round.
1998, seeded 9, won 5 matches, lost Goran Ivanisevic, semi-final.
1999, seeded 5, won 2 matches, lost Lorenzo Manta, 3rd round.
2000, seeded 11, won 1 match, lost Wayne Ferreira, 2nd round.
2001, did not play.
2002, unseeded, won 4 matches, lost Xavier Malisse, quarter-final.

Matches: 29–10; sets 98–42; games 813–653.

Longest Match: semi-final 1998, lost to Goran Ivanisevic 3–6 4–6 7–5 7–6 13–15 – a total of 72 games.

Age on winning singles: 24 years 214 days.

Overall Record:

	Titles	Matches Played	Won	Lost
Singles	1	39	29	10
Doubles	0	2	1	1
Mixed	0	0	0	0
Total	1	41	30	11

Career Achievements:
The Championships, Wimbledon: singles 1996.
Total Grand Slam titles: 1 – singles 1.
Netherlands Davis Cup team: 1991–1996, 1999, 2000, winning 7 from 15 matches (singles 6–8; doubles 1–0) in 9 ties.
Won: 17 singles titles, 3 doubles titles.
Played: 630 singles, winning 411.
Prize money: $10,077,425.

Full name: Richard Peter Krajicek
Born: 6th December, 1971, Rotterdam, Netherlands.

painted faces, determined to have a good time. It was a festive scene – as if the staid old Centre Court had lifted her skirts and danced the Can-Can. The Australian cricketers were there too. The entire Test team, fresh from victory over England in the first Test in Birmingham, had come to support Rafter.

What a final they gave us. It was a three hour epic of pure theatre, an emotional roller-coaster ride for both spectators and players. The injured Ivanisevic was desperate to become a Grand Slam winner at last, Rafter determined to make amends for his defeat twelve months earlier at the hands of Sampras who had admitted afterwards that the loss of the second set tie-break, which he had won 7–5, would probably have cost him the match.

The first three sets all turned on one break of serve and Ivanisevic was ahead 2–1 but as he closed in on immortality he faltered. Shattered by a call of footfault on a serve that would have been an ace he lost his self control, kicked his racket into the net, and found himself 2–3 down in the fourth. Another loss of serve cost him the set. For the moment Bad Goran had got the better of Good Goran, the alter egos he had introduced us to earlier in the meeting.

The tension and emotion in the fifth was, at times, overwhelming – both on and off the court. The wonder is that the two players could maintain such a high standard with the crowd erupting after almost every rally. Trailing 6–7, Ivanisevic was three times just two points from defeat. In the crisis his trusty serve did not fail him. Yet a few moments later, after breaking Rafter to lead 8–7, he double-faulted to go 15–30. Steadying himself, Goran levelled at 30–30 with a good serve and then unleashed his 27th ace of the match, his 213th of the tournament, to reach Championship point. The tension was unbearable. Everyone was on a knife edge.

Imagine the reaction as Goran delivered another double fault. Bedlam in the stands. With quiet restored he delivered another unreturnable serve. A second match point. Struggling to control his nerves, incredibly Goran followed with a third double-fault. Now rejoicing among the Rafter fans. They were hoping for a miracle as the Australian saved a third match point with an amazing lob. But the tennis gods did not oblige. Facing a fourth Championship point the exhausted Aussie tamely hit his backhand return into the net. Good Goran had finally triumphed.

The scenes that followed were exceptional. Goran lay flat on his face for a moment then shook hands with his opponent before climbing into the stands to embrace his father, whose heart condition had been seriously tested. Goran is still the only wild card ever to have won a Grand Slam title. He was the oldest champion since Connors in 1982 and the first left-hander to win since McEnroe in 1984.

To their credit, the Rafter fans were applauding Goran's win almost as fervently as the Croatians. Rafter himself was equally gracious. In his post match on-court interview he turned to Goran and said 'I'm happy for you mate'. A tear-

ful Goran had to compose himself before dedicating his win to his friend and fellow countryman Drazan Petrovic, the N.B.A. star who had been killed in a motoring accident in 1993.

The reception in Split when he returned home was extraordinary. Almost 200,000 people, two thirds of the entire population, turned out to welcome him. Goran was overcome. 'They said everybody who was not dead came to welcome me there. They came to welcome me and thank me that I gave them hope and joy those two weeks... And then I was partying for two days. Didn't sleep for four nights' he remembered.

To have climbed a personal Everest so late in his tennis life was the reward for years of effort and frustration. 'If I had lost in the final again it would have destroyed me' he said. 'I would probably have jumped off a bridge, or gone to live at the North Pole or something – anything just to disappear. Probably I would have killed myself because it would have destroyed everything. But now I am a happy man.'

There had been other, minor moments of happiness: carrying the Olympic flag in Barcelona in 1992 where his four successive five set victories were a record and his bronze medals in singles and doubles (with Goran Prpic) were the first Olympic medals won by his young country; reaching a career high ranking of No.2 in 1994; serving a record 1,477 aces in 1996 and leading the Tour in that department for six of his last ten years; reaching the semi-finals of the ATP Championships for the fourth time in 1996; winning his hometown tournament in Split for the ninth time in 1998, the most among his career collection of 22 singles and 9 doubles titles that earned him prize money of more than $19.8 million.

The frustrations were largely caused by the numerous injuries he had to contend with over the years. In 1993 it had been a stress fracture of his right foot; two years later he had undergone surgery on his right knee and in 1996 a stiff neck had forced him to retire to Agassi in the Miami final. In 1997 he had broken the middle finger of his right hand, an injury which sidelined him for two months, and in 1999 a back condition had forced his withdrawal from the Australian Open. For the whole of 2000 and 2001 he had played with a left shoulder that he knew required surgery. At last in May 2002 the operation to repair the rotator cuff was performed in Germany.

It allowed Goran to fulfil one last wish – to walk out on Centre Court once more as a defending champion. After two years absence for rehabilitation he returned to Wimbledon in 2004 for the last time and was duly acknowledged by his legion of fans. After reaching the third round he lost honourably to former champion Lleyton Hewitt and promptly announced his retirement from the Tour. It was fitting end to his playing career.

There would be one last bonus. In 2005 Croatia reached the final of the Davis Cup. Despite the fact that Goran was now playing only on the seniors Tour he was selected for the team that went to Bratislava for the final against the Slovak

Republic. Fittingly, the two men whose careers he had inspired, Ivan Ljubicic and Mario Ancic, won the trophy for Croatia amid universal rejoicing at home.

Goran at last felt fulfilled. During his years of struggle the media, inevitably, had dubbed him 'The Split Personality'. Today he is content with life. Apart from occasional appearances on the senior Tour he lives quietly with his wife, the former model Tatjana Dragovic, and their daughter Amber Maria in Zagreb. Literally and metaphorically Goran has come home.

Wimbledon Singles Record:

1988, unseeded, won 0 matches, lost Amos Mansdorf, 1st round.
1989, unseeded, won 1 match, lost Kenneth Flach, 2nd round.
1990, unseeded, won 5 matches, lost Boris Becker, semi-final.
1991, seeded 10, won 1 match, lost Nicholas Brown, 2nd round.
1992, seeded 8, won 6 matches, lost Andre Agassi, final.
1993, seeded 5, won 2 matches, lost Todd Martin, 3rd round.
1994, seeded 4, won 6 matches, lost Pete Sampras, final.
1995, seeded 4, won 5 matches, lost Pete Sampras, semi-final.
1996, seeded 4, won 4 matches, lost Jason Stoltenberg, quarter-final.
1997, seeded 2, won 1 match, lost Magnus Norman, 2nd round.
1998, seeded 14, won 6 matches, lost Pete Sampras, final.
1999, seeded 10, won 3 matches, lost Todd Martin, 4th round.
2000, unseeded, won 0 matches, lost Arnaud Clement, 1st round.
2001, unseeded, won 7 matches (*champion*) (sets 21–7 games 160–139).
2002, 2003, did not play.
2004, unseeded, won 2 matches, lost Lleyton Hewitt, 3rd round.

Matches: 49–14; sets 163–75; games 1349–1134.

Longest Match: Semi-final 1998, beat Richard Krajicek 6–3 6–4 5–7 6–7 15–13 – a total of 70 games.

Age on winning singles: 29 years, 299 days.

Overall Record:

	Titles	Matches		
		Played	Won	Lost
Singles	1	63	49	14
Doubles	0	10	5	5
Mixed	0	0	0	0
Total	1	73	54	19

Career Achievements:

The Championships, Wimbledon: singles 2001.
Total Grand Slam titles: 1 – singles 1.
Olympic Games: singles 1992, bronze; doubles 1992, bronze.
Yugoslavian Davis Cup team: 1988–1991, winning 15 from 19 matches (singles 8–3, doubles 7–1) in 8 ties.
Croatian Davis Cup team: 1993–2003, winning 33 from 44 matches (singles 20–6, doubles 13–5) in 18 ties.
Won: 22 singles titles, 9 doubles titles.
Played: 932 singles, winning 599.
Prize money: $19,876,579.

Full name: Goran Simun Ivanisevic
Born: 13th September, 1971, Split, Yugoslavia.

Lleyton Hewitt

2002

The Aussie Battler

The 1992 champion, Lleyton Hewitt, is the latest in a select band of Wimbledon winners whose strengths are deployed predominantly from the back of the court. Although the Australian is a perfectly competent volleyer, as were Dick Savitt (1951), Manuel Santana (1966), Jan Kodes (1973), Jimmy Connors (1974, 1982), Bjorn Borg (1976–1980) and Andre Agassi (1992), all of them preferred to dominate their opponents from the back of the court. All excelled as returners of the serve, all could pass and lob with precision, all felt secure in their domain astride the baseline.

While it has always been true that the nature of fast grass courts provides an advantage to players with strong serves and good volleys – 29 of Wimbledon's 36 post World War II winners fall into that category – it is also self evident that good ground strokes are an essential prerequisite to success on any surface. After all, even the best serve-and-volley experts must break an opponent's serve sometime if they are going to win. The speedy Hewitt who, like Connors, Borg and Agassi has a double-handed backhand, broke the serves and the hearts of so many opponents with his expertise on service return and pass.

When he had exploded on the scene in 1998 to win his first tournament as a feisty teenager, the world was put on notice to expect fireworks. Ever since, Lleyton has lived up to that reputation. His defeat of Andre Agassi and Jason Stoltenberg that memorable week in Adelaide to capture his home town tournament at the age of 16 years and 10 months still stands as one of the most extraordinary achievements of modern tennis. He was ranked a lowly 550 at the time. No-one lower ranked has ever won a tournament in Tour history and only one lad was younger when winning his first tournament. American Aaron Krickstein was just 16 years 2 months when he won at Tel Aviv in 1983.

Lleyton was coached originally by Peter Smith, whose son Luke would become the first Adelaide boy to win the NCAA Championships in America. Smith describes Lleyton's work ethic as outstanding. 'I've never seen anyone work so hard at that age' he said. ' Lleyton was always determined to succeed'. In 1999 Lleyton asked another home town man to help him achieve his lofty ambitions. In two short years Darren Cahill would guide young Lleyton to the very top of the game. When he ended 2001 as the No.1 player in the world he broke two records. He became the first Australian to reach that pinnacle since the rankings began in 1973; still only 20 years and eight months old he was also the youngest ever to head the rankings.

The highlight of that remarkable year, in which Lleyton captured six titles, was his first Grand Slam success at the US Open. His destruction of four-time champion Pete Sampras that blustery afternoon was clinical in its perfection. From the moment Hewitt broke serve in the opening game with three blistering returns, to the last stroke of that 7–6 6–1 6–1 execution – another winning backhand return of serve – he was letter perfect. Unaffected by the wind which was giving Sampras so much trouble he raced around the court at breakneck speed and pummelled the American relentlessly with winning returns and passes on both wings that at times seemed to defy the laws of physics. All the time you felt that the purple patch could not last. But it did. The longer the match went on – and it lasted a bare 114 minutes – the better Hewitt played. It was a *tour de force* that stamped the Aussie battler as a shot-maker of the highest class. That assessment was confirmed when, at the year's end in Sydney, he won the first of two back-to-back Masters titles for the loss of only one set.

Despite a bout of chicken pox that interrupted him early in 2002 Hewitt maintained his form well and became only the fourth man after Connors, Lendl and Sampras to remain in the top spot every week of the year. His Wimbledon triumph was no surprise. A third consecutive win at Queen's Club on the eve of The Championships presaged a good run. So it proved. Only once was he threatened, by Sjeng Schalken in their quarter-final. Having recovered from the loss of the first two sets the Dutchman missed a forehand pass on break point in the 11th game of the final set that would have given him the chance to serve for the match. Once he had escaped, Hewitt closed in on the title like a tiger pouncing on its prey. First Tim Henman, then surprise finalist David Nalbandian, who had beaten Belgium's Xavier Malisse in the other semi-final, were devoured in straight sets. It was further proof of Hewitt's growing maturity as a match player. It also signalled a change in the balance among the top men. Baseliners now predominated. Serve-and-volley players were becoming an endangered species.

Throughout his career Hewitt has been an outstanding competitor. Few men have been able to match his intensity. At the end of a particularly fierce rally he would bellow 'C'mon' as he pumped his fist and did a little skip of delight. It was no surprise to discover that Lleyton loved watching the Rocky movies.

Such in-your-face antics disturbed the purists who saw his behaviour as unnecessarily confrontational. Others saw it as the natural exuberance of a man who relied on an adrenalin rush to reach his peak. These attributes were at their most appropriate, and most effective in the cauldron of Davis Cup tennis where Hewitt played some of his finest matches. He was a member of the winning Australian team in 1999 that beat France in Nice, though he lost narrowly to Cedric Pioline in that one.

The following year Australia faced Brazil in the semi-finals. The match was played in Gustavo Kuerten's home town of Florianopolis, where the great man had never been beaten. Hewitt's 7–6, 6–3, 7–6 win over the three-time French Open champion was described by his captain John Fitzgerald as the finest-ever performance by an Australian in Davis Cup play – praise indeed from someone who knew his history and had witnessed the exploits of Rod Laver and Roy Emerson.

That year's final – a loss to the French on grass in Melbourne – left a little egg on Australian faces. Hewitt was beaten in that tie by Nicolas Escude in the opening match to set France off on their winning course. The defeat served only to strengthen Lleyton's determination to return to winning ways. The opportunity came two years later.

In the 2003 semi-final Australia had a home tie against Switzerland. The match was played on hard courts in Melbourne. On the opening day Hewitt faced Roger

Federer. The newly crowned Wimbledon champion swept through the first two sets and was within two points of victory in the third. This was the sort of challenge that Hewitt relished. Urged on by a patriotic Melbourne crowd the little Aussie embarked upon one of those great escapes that is still talked of in awe by those who witnessed it. His 5–7, 2–6, 7–6, 7–5, 6–1 victory was the foundation of an Australian win that pitted them against Spain in the final.

This was something of a grudge match because their loss to the Spaniards in Barcelona three years earlier had been accompanied by some behaviour from the Spanish captain and the crowd that John Newcombe, in his last year of captaincy for Australia, had described as unsporting and not in the spirit of Davis Cup tennis.

Again Hewitt set his country on the winning path. His victory over Juan Carlos Ferrero in the first match was the prelude to a 3–1 win.

Still in the middle of what is already an outstanding career, Lleyton has been unfortunate with injuries. After winning Sydney in January 2005 and then reaching the final of the Australian Open for the first time it seemed he was about to embark on another successful year. It was in his winning semi-final at Indian Wells against Andy Roddick that he first injured the big toe on his left foot that required surgery in March. Despite recurring problems he reached the semi-finals both at Wimbledon and the US Open where Federer beat him each time – just as he had done in the previous year's final at Flushing Meadows. Two weeks later a groin injury forced him to retire in the quarter-finals of Bangkok.

It was a clear signal that he needed to look after his body. Further surgery on his toe in October was followed by a fall at his home which left him with a broken rib. He would play no more tennis in 2005. The only consolation was that he now had a wife to look after him. Lleyton's marriage to Australian actress Bec Cartwright on 22nd of July at the Sydney Opera House was the social event of the year. Although he had recovered from his operation and injuries by the time the Masters Cup arrived in November, Lleyton was now concerned to be with Bec for the arrival of their first child. Mia Rebecca was born on 29th November as her father was training hard to make a successful return to the circuit in 2006.

The battle for supremacy between a rejuvenated Hewitt, a still improving Andy Roddick and the present ruler of men's tennis, Roger Federer, all of then being hotly challenged by some outstanding youngsters like Rafael Nadal, Richard Gasquet, Gael Monfils, Tomas Berdych and Andy Murray promises a bright future.

Wimbledon Singles Record:
1999, unseeded, won 2 matches, lost Boris Becker, 3rd round.
2000, seeded 7, won 0 matches, lost Jan-Michael Gambill, 1st round.
2001, seeded 5, won 3 matches, lost Nicolas Escude, 4th round.
2002, seeded 1, won 7 matches, *champion*, (sets 21–2, games 139–78).
2003, seeded 1, won 0 matches, lost Ivo Karlovic, 1st round.

2004, seeded 7, won 4 matches, lost Roger Federer, quarter-final.

2005, seeded 3, won 5 matches, lost Roger Federer, semi-final.

Matches: 21–6; sets 67–27; games 517–393.

Longest Match: 4th round 2001, lost to Nicolas Escude, 6–4 4–6 3–6 6–4 4–6 – a total of 49 games.

Age on winning singles: 21 years, 153 days.

Overall Record:

	Titles	Matches Played	Won	Lost
Singles	1	27	21	6
Doubles	0	3	2	1
Mixed	0	6	5	1
Total	1	36	28	8

Career Achievements:

The Championships, Wimbledon: singles 2002.

US Championships: singles 2001, doubles 2000.

Total Grand Slam titles: 3 – singles 2, doubles 1.

Year end Championships: singles 2001, 2002.

Australian Davis Cup team: 1999–2005, winning 30 from 38 matches (singles 27–6, doubles 3–2) in 20 ties.

Won: 33 singles titles, 2 doubles titles.

Played: 517 singles, winning 398.

Prize money: $20,232,573.

Full name: Lleyton Glynn Hewitt

Born: 24th February, 1981, Adelaide, South Australia, Australia.

Roger Federer

2003, 2004, 2005

Switzerland's Supercharged Superstar

The career of Roger Federer is a work in progress. Already by the close of 2005, still only 24, the Swiss superstar had enjoyed more success than most mortals dream of achieving in a lifetime.

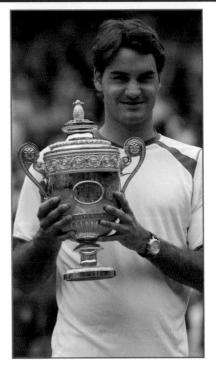

Consider the bare facts. Among his haul of 33 tournament wins Federer has won his first six Grand Slam finals, a feat last achieved in the 19th century in the days of the Challenge Round; he won 24 consecutive tournament finals between October 2003 and October 2005 (a phenomenal achievement that is exactly double the previous record of 12, achieved by both Bjorn Borg and John McEnroe in their glory years); for the second year in a row he won 11 titles, losing only six matches in 2004 and four in 2005; he has twice won back-to-back Wimbledon and US Open titles, a double achieved only twice – by Bill Tilden in the 1920s and Donald Budge in the 1930s; he put together a winning streak of 35 matches in 2005, a figure exceeded only once in the open era – by Guillermo Vilas who had 46 wins in 1977; his winning run of 40 matches on hard courts, still alive at the end of 2005, is another open era record.

By any measure these are awesome achievements. However, when you think about it they are not altogether surprising for there was early evidence that Roger had exceptional talent. In 1998 he won the junior singles and doubles titles at Wimbledon (only two others have done that), as well as the Orange Bowl 18s title. That year he was crowned the World Junior Champion. At Wimbledon in 2001, aged 19, he beat seven-time champion Sampras in the fourth round. Two years later he joined Bjorn Borg, Pat Cash and Stefan Edberg as Wimbledon's only junior champions who went on the win the men's singles.

What is it about the man that has made him so exceptional? A natural athlete, Roger's speed of thought and movement, when allied to an abundant talent with the racket, give him options that others envy. Having built up his physical strength since his junior days he can now improvise as the occasion demands, firing winners on forehand and backhand, volley and lob, serve and smash, almost at will. Perhaps his two finest weapons are his serve and his forehand. Both are hit with easy grace; both are deadly. A strong right wrist allows him to apply fizzing topspin on the forehand when necessary to create sharp angles; it also produces heavy slice or top-spin on the serve.

During 2004 and 2005 the confidence factor lifted Roger to another level. He had learned how to adjust his tactics during a match without panicking, which used to happen occasionally in his junior days when frustration at his inability to produce shots that he knew he possessed made him angry.

Not until the close of 2003 did the realisation dawn that he was the equal of any member of the top ten. By winning the Tennis Masters Cup in Houston with a straight sets victory over Andre Agassi in the final after saving two match points against the American at the round-robin stage, the weight of expectation upon him as the new Wimbledon champion was lifted. Now he felt he belonged among the elite. He spent the next two years proving it.

Remarkably in 2004 he had travelled without a coach, having parted amicably from Peter Lundgren who had coached him to his first Wimbledon win the year before. Equally remarkable was the fact that having won three Grand Slams that year, he decided to ask Tony Roche to coach him at all the major events in 2005. It hardly seemed necessary.

Throughout this time, however, he has been loyally supported on the road by his long-time girlfriend, Miroslava Varinek and by his trainer, Pavel Kovak. 'Mirka' has helped him to mature and with growing maturity has come stature. Without a hint of conceit Federer can now explain why he is better than other players. He can discuss dispassionately his feelings as the world No.1. Going into 2006 he had headed the rankings for a total of 101 weeks and had been in the top spot every week of 2005 – another of those records. This one he shares with Ivan Lendl, Jimmy Connors, Pete Sampras and Lleyton Hewitt.

Watching Federer's development as a match player, and noting his happy knack of finding a winning formula when he is not at his best, there is the unmis-takable feeling that we may be witnessing the evolution of the greatest striker of a tennis ball who ever lived. As with Sampras there is one piece still missing before that assessment can be universally accepted. Roger still needs to prove himself a champion on clay by winning the French Open. Again, like Sampras, Roger has been in the semi-finals at Roland Garros but unlike the great American, whose 1994 win in Rome was his only clay court success, he has already won five tour-naments on the surface. His future battles against the young Spanish left-hander Rafael Nadal, the current King of Clay, who beat him in Paris in 2005, will be matches to savour.

Popular wherever he goes, Federer has shown remarkable awareness of the need to support and promote the tournaments which give him his livelihood. He may have taken more than $20 million from the game in prize money, a sum that already places him in seventh place in the all-time list of career earnings, but he is more than willing to put in the time and effort to contribute to the growth and future success of the sport he loves.

He is also a man with a social conscience. In South Africa, the country of his mother's birth, he has set up a Foundation to help underprivileged youngsters and visits the country whenever he can. Inevitably for one so talented, so successful and so popular, awards have come his way from all quarters. The Laureus Award, the ATP Player of the Year Award, the Swiss Athlete of the Year Award, BBC television's Overseas Sports Personality of the Year Award – you name it, he's won it.

More that anything else, at a time when the game was in danger of dying of boredom because of the monotonous one dimensional nature of the sport – too many players hitting too much topspin – Federer has reminded us all how beautiful this game can be – if you are good enough. He is. Let us hope that other young men of talent will be inspired to follow his example.

Wimbledon Singles Record:
1999, unseeded, won 0 matches, lost Jiri Novak, 1st round.
2000, unseeded, won 0 matches, lost Yevgeny Kafelnikov, 1st round.
2001, seeded 15, won 4 matches, lost Tim Henman, quarter-final.
2002, seeded 7, won 0 matches, lost Mario Ancic, 1st round.
2003, seeded 4, won 7 matches, *champion*, (sets 21–1, games 136–81).
2004, seeded 1, won 7 matches, *champion*, (sets 21–2, games 141–78).
2005, seeded 1, won 7 matches, *champion*, (sets 21–1, games 138–85).

Matches: 25–4; sets 78–20; games 583–406.

Longest Match: 4th round 2001, beat Pete Sampras 7–6 5–7 6–4 6–7 7–5 – a total of 60 games.

Age on first winning singles: 21 years 332 days.

Age on last winning singles: 23 years 329 days.

Overall Record:

	Titles	Matches Played	Won	Lost
Singles	3	29	25	4
Doubles	0	9	7	2
Mixed	0	0	0	0
Total	3	38	32	6

Career Achievements:
The Championships, Wimbledon: singles 2003–2005.
US Championships: singles 2004, 2005.
Australian Championships: singles 2004.
Total Grand Slam titles: 6 – singles 6.
Year end Championships: singles 2003, 2004.
Swiss Davis Cup team: 1999–2005, winning 28 from 38 matches (singles 20–6; doubles 8–4) in 14 ties.
Won: 24 singles titles, 7 doubles titles.
Played: 511 singles, winning 391.
Prize money: $15,962,457.

Full name: Roger Federer
Born: 8th August, 1981, Basle, Switzerland.

Gentlemen's Singles Finals

1877–2005

From 1878 until 1921 the holder of the Gentlemen's Singles Championship did not compete until the Challenge Round, when he met the winner of the All Comers' Singles to decide The Championship. When the holder did not defend his title the winner of the All Comers' Singles automatically became Champion and the years this occurred are marked by an asterisk.

```
 1877  Spencer Gore bt William Marshall 6–1 6–2 6–4
 1878  Frank Hadow bt Spencer Gore 7–5 6–1 9–7
★1879  John Hartley bt Vere St. Leger Goold 6–2 6–4 6–2
 1880  John Hartley bt Herbert Lawford 6–3 6– 2–6 6–3
 1881  William Renshaw bt John Hartley 6–0 6–1 6–1
 1882  William Renshaw bt Ernest Renshaw 6–1 2–6 6–4 6–2 6–2
 1883  William Renshaw bt Ernest Renshaw 2–6 6–3 6–3 4–6 6–3
 1884  William Renshaw bt Herbert Lawford 6–0 6–4 9–7
 1885  William Renshaw bt Herbert Lawford 7–5 6–2 4–6 7–5
 1886  William Renshaw bt Herbert Lawford 6–0 5–7 6–3 6–4
★1887  Herbert Lawford bt Ernest Renshaw 1–6 6–3 3–6 6–4 6–4
 1888  Ernest Renshaw bt Herbert Lawford 6–3 7–5 6–0
 1889  William Renshaw bt Ernest Renshaw 6–1 6–1 3–6 6–0
 1890  Willoby Hamilton bt William Renshaw 6–8 6–2 3–6 6–1 6–1
★1891  Wilfred Baddeley bt Joshua Pim 6–1 1–6 7–5 6–0
 1892  Wilfred Baddeley bt Joshua Pim 4–6 6–3 6–3 6–2
 1893  Joshua Pim bt Wilfred Baddeley 3–6 6–1 6–3 6–2
 1894  Johsua Pim bt Wilfred Baddeley 10–8 6–2 8–6
★1895  Wilfred Baddeley bt Wilberforce Eaves 4–6 2–6 8–6 6–2 6–3
 1896  Harold Mahony bt Wilfred Baddeley 6–2 6–8 5–7 8–6 6–3
 1897  Reginald Doherty bt Harold Mahony 6–4 6–4 6–3
 1898  Reginald Doherty bt Laurence Doherty 6–3 6–3 2–6 5–7 6–1
 1899  Reginald Doherty bt Arthur Gore 1–6 4–6 6–3 6–3 6–3
 1900  Reginald Doherty bt Sidney Smith 6–8 6–3 6–1 6–2
 1901  Arthur Gore bt Reginald Doherty 4–6 7–5 6–4 6–4
 1902  Laurence Doherty bt Arthur Gore 6–4 6–3 3–6 6–0
 1903  Laurence Doherty bt Frank Riseley 7–5 6–3 6–0
 1904  Laurence Doherty bt Frank Riseley 6–1 7–5 8–6
 1905  Laurence Doherty bt Norman Brookes 8–6 6–2 6–4
```

1906 Laurence Doherty bt Frank Riseley 6–4 4–6 6–2 6–3
★1907 Norman Brookes bt Arthur Gore 6–4 6–2 6–2
★1908 Arthur Gore bt Roper Barrett 6–3 6–2 4–6 3–6 6–4
1909 Arthur Gore bt Major Ritchie 6–8 1–6 6–2 6–2 6–2
1910 Anthony Wilding bt Arthur Gore 6–4 7–5 4–6 6–2
1911 Anthony Wilding bt Roper Barrett 6–4 4–6 2–6 6–2 ret'd
1912 Anthony Wilding bt Arthur Gore 6–4 6–4 4–6 6–4
1913 Anthony Wilding bt Maurice McLoughlin 8–6 6–3 10–8
1914 Norman Brookes bt Anthony Wilding 6–4 6–4 7–5
1915–1918 not held
1919 Gerald Patterson bt Norman Brookes 6–3 7–5 6–2
1920 William Tilden bt Gerald Patterson 2–6 6–3 6–2 6–4
1921 William Tilden bt Brian Norton 4–6 2–6 6–1 6–0 7–5
1922 Gerald Patterson bt Randolph Lycett 6–3 6–4 6–2
1923 William Johnston bt Francis Hunter 6–0 6–3 6–1
1924 Jean Borotra bt Rene Lacoste 6–1 3–6 6–1 3–6 6–4
1925 Rene Lacoste bt Jean Borotra 6–3 6–3 4–6 8–6
1926 Jean Borotra bt Howard Kinsey 8–6 6–1 6–3
1927 Henri Cochet bt Jean Borotra 4–6 4–6 6–3 6–4 7–5
1928 Rene Lacoste bt Henri Cochet 6–1 4–6 6–4 6–2
1929 Henri Cochet bt Jean Borotra 6–4 6–3 6–4
1930 William Tilden bt Wilmer Allison 6–3 9–7 6–4
1931 Sidney Wood w.o. Frank Shields
1932 Ellsworth Vines bt Bunny Austin 6–4 6–2 6–0
1933 Jack Crawford bt Ellsworth Vines 4–6 11–9 6–2 2–6 6–4
1934 Fred Perry bt Jack Crawford 6–3 6–0 7–5
1935 Fred Perry bt Gottfried von Cramm 6–2 6–4 6–4
1936 Fred Perry bt Gottfried von Cramm 6–1 6–1 6–0
1937 Donald Budge bt Gottfried von Cramm 6–3 6–4 6–2
1938 Donald Budge bt Bunny Austin 6–1 6–0 6–3
1939 Bobby Riggs bt Elwood Cooke 2–6 8–6 3–6 6–3 6–2
1940–1945 not held
1946 Yvon Petra bt Geoffrey Brown 6–2 6–4 7–9 5–7 6–4
1947 Jack Kramer bt Thomas Brown 6–1 6–3 6–2
1948 Bob Falkenburg bt John Bromwich 7–5 0–6 6–2 3–6 7–5
1949 Ted Schroeder bt Jaroslav Drobny 3–6 6–0 6–3 4–6 6–4
1950 Budge Patty bt Frank Sedgman 6–1 8–10 6–2 6–3
1951 Richard Savitt bt Ken McGregor 6–4 6–4 6–4
1952 Frank Sedgman bt Jaroslav Drobny 4–6 6–2 6–3 6–2
1953 Vic Seixas bt Kurt Nielsen 9–7 6–3 6–4
1954 Jaroslav Drobny bt Ken Rosewall 13–11 4–6 6–2 9–7

1955 Tony Trabert bt Kurt Nielsen 6–3 7–5 6–1

1956 Lew Hoad bt Ken Rosewall 6–2 4–6 7–5 6–4

1957 Lew Hoad bt Ashley Cooper 6–2 6–1 6–2

1958 Ashley Cooper bt Neale Fraser 3–6 6–3 6–4 13–11

1959 Alex Olmedo bt Rod Laver 6–4 6–3 6–4

1960 Neale Fraser bt Rod Laver 6–4 3–6 9–7 7–5

1961 Rod Laver bt Charles McKinley 6–3 6–1 6–4

1962 Rod Laver bt Martin Mulligan 6–2 6–2 6–1

1963 Charles McKinley bt Fred Stolle 9–7 6–1 6–4

1964 Roy Emerson bt Fred Stolle 6–4 12–10 4–6 6–3

1965 Roy Emerson bt Fred Stolle 6–2 6–4 6–4

1966 Manuel Santana bt Dennis Ralston 6–4 11–9 6–4

1967 John Newcombe bt Wilhelm Bungert 6–3 6–1 6–1

1968 Rod Laver bt Tony Roche 6–3 6–4 6–2

1969 Rod Laver bt John Newcombe 6–4 5–7 6–4 6–4

1970 John Newcombe bt Ken Rosewall 5–7 6–3 6–2 3–6 6–1

1971 John Newcombe bt Stan Smith 6–3 5–7 2–6 6–4 6–4

1972 Stan Smith bt Ilie Nastase 4–6 6–3 6–3 4–6 7–5

1973 Jan Kodes bt Alexander Metreveli 6–1 9–8(7–5) 6–3

1974 Jimmy Connors bt Ken Rosewall 6–1 6–1 6–4

1975 Arthur Ashe bt Jimmy Connors 6–1 6–1 5–7 6–4

1976 Bjorn Borg bt Ilie Nastase 6–4 6–2 9–7

1977 Bjorn Borg bt Jimmy Connors 3–6 6–2 6–1 5–7 6–4

1978 Bjorn Borg bt Jimmy Connors 6–2 6–2 6–3

1979 Bjorn Borg bt Roscoe Tanner 6–7(4–7) 6–1 3–6 6–3 6–4

1980 Bjorn Borg bt John McEnroe 1–6 7–5 6–3 6–7(16–18) 8–6

1981 John McEnroe bt Bjorn Borg 4–6 7–6(7–1) 7–6(7–4) 6–4

1982 Jimmy Connors bt John McEnroe 3–6 6–3 6–7(2–7) 7–6(7–5) 6–4

1983 John McEnroe bt Chris Lewis 6–2 6–2 6–2

1984 John Mc Enroe bt Jimmy Connors 6–1 6–1 6–2

1985 Boris Becker bt Kevin Curren 6–3 6–7(4–7) 7–6(7–3) 6–4

1986 Boris Becker bt Ivan Lendl 6–4 6–3 7–5

1987 Pat Cash bt Ivan Lendl 7–6(7–5) 6–2 7–5

1988 Stefan Edberg bt Boris Becker 4–6 7–6(7–2) 6–4 6–2

1989 Boris Becker bt Stefan Edberg 6–0 7–6(7–1) 6–4

1990 Stefan Edberg bt Boris Becker 6–2 6–2 3–6 3–6 6–4

1991 Michael Stich bt Boris Becker 6–4 7–6(7–4) 6–4

1992 Andre Agassi bt Goran Ivanisevic 6–7(8–10) 6–4 6–4 1–6 6–4

1993 Pete Sampras bt Jim Courier 7–6(7–3) 7–6(8–6) 3–6 6–3

1994 Pete Sampras bt Goran Ivanisevic 7–6(7–2) 7–6(7–5) 6–0

1995 Pete Sampras bt Boris Becker 6–7(5–7) 6–2 6–4 6–2

1996 Richard Krajicek bt MaliVai Washington 6–3 6–4 6–3
1997 Pete Sampras bt Cedric Pioline 6–4 6–2 6–4
1998 Pete Sampras bt Goran Ivanisevic 6–7(2–7) 7–6(11–9) 6–4 3–6 6–2
1999 Pete Sampras bt Andre Agassi 6–3 6–4 7–5
2000 Pete Sampras bt Pat Rafter 6–7(10–12) 7–6(7–5) 6–4 6–2
2001 Goran Ivanisevic bt Pat Rafter 6–3 3–6 6–3 2–6 9–7
2002 Lleyton Hewitt bt David Nalbandian 6–1 6–3 6–2
2003 Roger Federer bt Mark Philippoussis 7–6(7–5) 6–2 7–6(7–3)
2004 Roger Federer bt Andy Roddick 4–6 7–5 7–6(7–3) 6–4
2005 Roger Federer bt Andy Roddick 6–2 7–6 (7–2) 6–4

Index of Champions